(continued from front flap)

but which are built into the flesh and blood of the young." These are the problems of physical and spiritual survival in a world haunted by the bomb and the frozen politics of a dying class.

Mr. Spender's narrative is concrete and humane and his interpretation is clear-eyed in the manner of Orwell's *Homage to Catalonia.* His judgments are informed by common sense and by a decent respect for what remains of our civilized traditions. He has profound sympathy for the struggles of the young to make a world in which they can not only survive but where they can live with honor and in keeping with the ideals by which they measure and find wanting the world they have fallen heir to.

Jacket design by Bob Korn

Random House, Inc., New York, N.Y. 10022. Publishers of THE RANDOM HOUSE DICTIONARY OF THE ENGLISH LANGUAGE: the Unabridged and College Editions, The Modern Library and Vintage Books

Books by Stephen Spender:

World Within World
Collected Poems
Selected Poems
The Destructive Element
The Creative Element
European Witness
Engaged in Writing

The Year of the Young Rebels

RANDOM HOUSE · NEW YORK

STEPHEN SPENDER

The Year
of the
Young Rebels

Contents

Acknowledgements

My thanks are due to Mr Jan Kavan for allowing me to quote from his writings and for talking to me about the Czech students; to Miss Mary McCarthy for reading some of the material and making very helpful comments; to Mr David Griffith, the editor of *Student* (Amsterdam), for sending me transcripts of taped conversations with students of the *Freie Universität*; to Monsieur Claude Roy for his encouragement and for lending me his copy of Voline's *La Révolution Inconnue;* to Mr Jason Epstein for his valuable suggestions; and to all the authors and publishers from whose works I have quoted.

The excerpt from Allen Ginsberg's poem *Howl* which appears on page 137 is reproduced by permission of Messrs McBride & Broadley.

The Columbia Happenings

On 23 April 1968 I went to the offices of *Rat* in East 20th Street, to meet the editor, Jeffrey Shero. They were in a wind-swept, dust-and-dirt blown area of New York, in a wide street with very miscellaneous shops along one block, and large blank tenements beyond the intersections. *Rat's* offices were humanised – animalised – by the poster of a rat holding a gun, by the two trash cans confronting me as soon as I opened the front door, and by the litter of pamphlets, books, magazines on tables, in a large room with an inner office screened off.

Jef Shero was in his early twenties and had a blond beard and light eyes. As soon as he came back to his office (he had been out when I arrived) he greeted me with the words: 'We've taken Columbia. We've liberated the president's offices. Our next number will be a real blockbuster. We'll publish the captured enemy documents.'

He suggested that we go to Columbia at once. I called a taxi and on our way asked him questions. He talked in a manner that showed he thought most people's ideas and attitudes to be simple projections of their material circumstances. The professors at Columbia (maybe some of them are liberals and think they sympathise with the students, but still) had acquired interests that conditioned them in such a way that their views were those of the administration which gave them tenure and status, and supported their families. As soon as a young man stops being a student (Jef went on) and becomes an instructor or assistant he starts absorbing the interests of the university, especially when he marries and begins to have a family. The students – i.e. the young – were different from the faculty because their interests had not as yet become one with those of the university.

This line of thought was scarcely new to me, since it was pretty much what my own generation thought when we were young. We visualised a propertied social class the great majority of whose members were conditioned in attitudes and thinking by their interests. We observed with malicious pleasure, when we

3

saw it happen to others – with guilt when we saw it happen to ourselves – how class interests could influence the individual, without his recognising it; so that love of gardening, the most refined aesthetic taste, altruistic idealism, belief in absolute justice or objective truth, and – especially this – the capacity of the liberal to see two sides of every question, were subtle defences of the individual's own interest, a self-deceiving refusal to be on the side of those without property or class material interests.

When Jef Shero used a term such as 'fink' to describe a hypocritical self-defensive liberal, it was a cap fitting some person or attitude I had known thirty years before. During the coming weeks of talking with students I was often to suspect that part of the fascination was not that of hearing ideas that were new, but nostalgic ideas springing from new lips, atonal variations on old themes.

We arrived at Columbia and walked on to the huge grey gently sloping campus. It was crowded with students who seemed at once agitated and aimless, clustered in groups, or walking against the background of grandiose buildings, architectural repertoires of Athens and Rome, the Renaissance. There was an April sky of blue and white and the first spray of spring clung around the branches of trees like green mist. Some of the students and faculty members were being harangued, by what I suppose were rebel speakers, from the steps of the long columned mausoleum-like Hamilton Hall, or round the stubby Sun Dial.

I walked over to Low Library, from the second floor window of which (or the first floor, by English counting) hung a placard on which was written JOIN US. On the sill, students were standing, or seated dangling their legs. They were dark scruffy figures, bearded men, girls with hair like sea weed. Below the sill there was another window reaching almost to the ground and covered with an iron grid which looked as easy to climb as ladders glued together.

Jef said: 'Why don't you join them?' I hesitated, fink-like thoughts battling in my head. I knew little or nothing of their reasons for being there, so should not join them on an impulse of sympathy, just to please. To support them might immensely irritate professors I knew at Columbia, who would rightly think

4

this no business of mine. On the other hand I wanted to know, to see and hear them. I was a writer intending to write about this and if I was restrained by scruples from seeing the scene, I had better give up all thought of doing so. I climbed the grid, was helped up by the students on the sill, and found myself standing in President Kirk's office.

After the brilliant light outside it seemed dark, with bulky furniture, a very large table or desk, shadowy figures, girls and boys, both with long hair, beards, jackets, open-neck shirts, belts, jeans, some medallions hanging from some necks. A few of the students held carton cups in their hands from which they sipped soft drinks. 'Have one of the president's cigars,' someone said, and I declined, sign that I was not taking their side. The door of the office was open and led to a corridor in which there were other groups of students standing, talking. Beyond this a door opened into a further room where there was a meeting going on. Someone explained: 'We are democratically deciding whether (a) to leave the building free of access; (b) to barricade ourselves in; or (c) whether or not to put up resistance if we are attacked.'

They considered each of these propositions in turn, making speeches for and against, and taking votes. A few minutes later the meeting ended and they drifted along the corridor and into President Kirk's office, the decision having been made to barricade. Someone across the room asked me if this was like Spain. The question took me back mentally to another scene: the University of Madrid over thirty years ago. The Castroite group of several of the students even provided a hispanic touch. What I remembered was a large lecture theatre with lines of seats stepped down to the well of a platform. High up in the room there were men in the slack uniforms of the Spanish militia. Some of them were reading books. Unlike the students here, they were using the university as a university while making their revolution. On the platform was a putrefying corpse. It could not be moved because through a window above the platform it was in the line of fire from the window of a building across the way, occupied by the Falangists.

In the presidential office the mood was so intense that I had little doubt that if it had been Spain – if there had been the enemy firing at them from an adjoining building – most of those present

5

would have been the militia. Some of them were rehearsing a revolution with such passion that their roles would have become real in a revolutionary situation. I went later to another building where there were offices with telephones and switchboards. There was a fevered atmosphere of transmitting and receiving messages, writing names and instructions on sheets of paper, again reminding me of Spain, of an office in Barcelona where I had seen young officers yelling instructions down the telephone to comrades waiting at the other end of the line.

A friend in New York had warned me that it would be useless for me to talk with Tom Hayden, the SDS (Students for a Democratic Society) leader, because he had nothing to say to anyone over thirty. So when I stumbled into him in the president's rooms, all I can remember of our conversation (he was very polite) was my asking him 'How old are you?' and his answering 'Twenty-nine' – which I found reassuring. I still felt too uneasy, though, to talk, but I keep my impression of him – with his slightly scarred complexion and his light eyes – as a general visiting a battlefield. When I got home I read in his remarkably ordered and almost military account of the July 1967 Newark riots, entitled *Rebellion in Newark*:[1]

These tactics of disorder will be defined by the authorities as criminal anarchy. But it may be that disruption will create possibilities of meaningful change. This depends on whether the leaders of ghetto struggles can be more successful in building a strong organisation than they have been so far. Violence can contribute to shattering the status quo but only politics and organisation can transform it. In order to build a more decent community while resisting racist power, more than violence is required. People need to create self-government. We are at a point where democracy—the idea and practice of people controlling their lives – is a revolutionary issue in the United States.

Tom Hayden seems the outstanding example of the radicalised student leader – his radicalisation began in the early Sixties at Berkeley where he was influenced by the disorders. But there were better reasons for it. In 1962 he was jailed in Albany, Georgia, for his support of coloured people. Tom

[1] Tom Hayden, *Rebellion in Newark*, New York (Random) 1968.

6

Hayden's presence in President Low's offices was paralleled by that of the black power leader Stokely Carmichael at Hamilton Hall.

Columbia was then a 'scene' on which forces from outside converged. As we shall see, the blacks were more the representatives of these forces than belonging to the university. Jef Shero's very appropriately named *Rat* represented the underground on the campus. This surfaces not so much as ideas – though there are revolutionary ones – as through language, or rather through two languages. One language might be called Dialogue. It is the language of the young painfully and rather incoherently trying to explain themselves, knowing that a professor is reading over their shoulder. Secretly they want to pass his examination standards. Here, by Paul Millman in *Rat* (September 1968), is a specimen of Dialogue:

... The siege of Columbia was the first time that any part of these developing middle-class rebels rejected outright a *promise* for liberal, peaceful change. Once again America (in this case through Columbia University) held open the promise of negotiating away some of its power. This time, however, the full significance of that promise was understood. It had been held out many times before to the Columbia students. Each time they found that, even if superficial concessions were made, conditions didn't change.

This language attempts to be reasonable. Quite a lot of *Rat* is written in this serious vein of considered opinion and reporting about America, France, Germany, and also Czechoslovakia. But *Rat* (and a whole number of other magazines – *Los Angeles Free Press, Washington Free Press, New York Free Press*, and in England the *International Times* and the *Black Dwarf*) has quite another style, which may be termed 'underground'. The 'underground' is not just literary, it is also illustrative (pop art), musical (pop), fashion (dress), which shows in the layout and the very look of these papers. The underground style is irreverent, disrespectful, uninhibited, informal, yet very expressive. This style, which began with the Beatniks and which continues through Pop, is based on speaking the unspeakable. It is a style of protest, the basic protest being against censorship: not just official censorship but social censorship which inhibits you from

7

saying anything you like to anyone anywhere. For its fashion-
ables it connects personal permissiveness about sex and drugs
with the revolution (whether the revolution could tolerate it for
long is another matter), as is shown in this paragraph from the
Los Angeles Free Press:[1]

Dope smoking clearly shows the space between the generations.
It distinguishes 'young from old'. It is the most obvious sign,
for those who need one, of the Revolution. Dope smoking continues, increases, while the law, broken so casually, is reduced to
horseshit.

Much of the correspondence in *Rat* is written in 'underground'

What difference can there be between shoving liberty up the ass of
Vietnam and giving America love in the same way? (When you're
up against a wall the gun may loom larger than the man and a
penis without human context loses the power of creation.)

This makes me think of the New York garbage strike which
took place at almost the same time as the Columbia riots. Food,
and God knows what else, rotted uncollected on the sidewalk.
One steered one's way precariously through odours thick as
soup. Ordures, material which is usually overlooked, avoided,
not mentioned, left in the gutter has been absorbed into language,
into the discourse of students, and even into the unwashed,
unshaven tattered materials out of which they have made a
fashion. It asserts their insistence on using an idiom which is
insulting, moment by moment and phrase by phrase, to the
academic, the conventional, the responsible. Because this permits so much to be said that previously had been filtered into
technical, physiological or psychological jargon, it undermines
any language of good manners, polite forms and evasive
euphemisms. In this it is certainly revolutionary, and with
the young one is constantly brought up against the prospect
of a future which will discard the past as the language and
style of Roman mercenaries discarded the manners of high Latin.

Underground culture was certainly one of the forces that
had flooded into the Columbia campus, and Mark Rudd the
student leader was as we shall see, one of its virtuosi.

[1] John Rosevear, 'Dope Smoking – the state of Art', *Los Angeles Free Press*,
June 14, 1968.

A few days later I got a further impression of the tense nervous 'revolutionary' seriousness of the students when I went late one evening to a meeting of architectural students in a classroom of one of the 'liberated' buildings. They sat on the floor listening with total attention to an extremely incoherent speaker – a non-verbal type – who was explaining the negotiations between the students occupying this building with those occupying other buildings and with the faculty. A matter much discussed was 'amnesty'. If the administration accepted amnesty they legitimised such mutinous acts as the imprisonment of Mr Coleman, Dean of Columbia College, in his office and the impending publication in *Rat* of the president's papers; if the students abandoned it they were casting their most audacious leaders to gnashing authorities. During the stumbling proposals reported by the speaker (these included the idea that all the students should accept the same symbolic punishment) my thoughts strayed to white-haired liberal professors whom I imagined standing like guardian angels in the dark outside.

But their meeting was not amusing. An overwhelming piece of evidence arguing the seriousness of it all was the fact that they scarcely slept. The students were sleepless (and so were the professors), and they did not eat much either. Nor, for that matter, did the students at the Sorbonne, as I was to discover a month later.

In an interview published in *Partisan Review* (Summer 1968), Lionel Trilling said, rather apologetically, that all he could recall of his feelings during those weeks was that he had a great many of them, and they were all intense. 'Very likely my present neutralised state is the result of fatigue,' he declared.

The uprisings, in New York, Paris, and Berlin had an absorbing trance-like quality, like a shared hallucination. Professor F. W. Dupee writes:

The euphoria . . . was no overnight phenomenon. It persisted beyond the first dramatic hours in Low [library], consolidated itself as a political force on the campus, became a contagion, spread to large numbers of students and younger teachers who, I would guess, by normal temper and conviction, were scarcely to be identified with the fanatical few. In other words, what had originated as a demonstration began to assume in their minds the stature of a revolution – a power seizure effected within a single institution which they regarded as a microcosm of the whole society. True, this delusion – as I fear it must be called – was unwittingly encouraged by the grim intransigence of the central Administration, which, becoming virtually invisible, refused to negotiate with the rebels 'under coercion', threatening police action, was like an embattled government-in-exile.[1]

At the Sorbonne there was even more of this feeling of shadow revolutionary forces debating in their committees, occupying buildings, orating, building barricades. Observers there too noted the sleeplessness of the students who, sitting up and discussing all night and eating little, became more and more wraithlike. Abstention from sleep and food was not entirely the result of there being so much to do. It was all part of a revolution rehearsal, like a war game. It helped them prove to themselves and others their seriousness, and they took themselves seriously. But when they began to lay claims to real seriousness the question of their values becomes pressing. For instance, when students said, as they did at Columbia, the Sorbonne, the *Freie Universität* and at English Art Schools, that more work had been done there during the weeks of revolution and occupation than ever before, their claim throws doubts on their understanding of what is meant by work – or even by revolution. It is like saying that revolutionaries work more seriously than scholars. What is true, of course, is that 'participation' in a rehearsal for revolution released energy and intelligence in students who had previously seemed uncooperative and torpid. Some of their teachers (particularly at the Sorbonne) noticed this, and reflected that there was perhaps something to be learned here by educators.

Historic Issues

Making their revolution while they are at the same time living the revolutionary life, the rebellious students were almost pedantically insistent on historic events, crucial issues, pregnant dates. The reader of their pamphlets and articles may well feel dismayed by the sense of being plunged into text book history, in which he has to learn by heart the Key Grievance, the Catalystic episode.

[1] F. W. Dupee, 'The Uprising at Columbia', *New York Review of Books*, September 26, 1968.

These have the classical look of classroom examples such as the Cause of the Indian Mutiny; which, if I remember rightly, arose from the introduction by the British into the Indian army of the Enfield rifle, with cartridges which had to be greased at one end (which?) with pig's fat, and then bitten when loading; to the abysmal defilement of the Bengali sepoys.

The issues are symptomatic of each movement. The German students, for example, tend to choose occasions for protest which dramatise theoretic lectures on class conflict or the struggle against imperialism. Thus in June 1967, on the occasion of the state visit of the Shah of Iran to the Federal Republic, they made a great demonstration outside the Berlin Opera House, when the Shah was attending a performance of *The Magic Flute* put on for his entertainment (an odd choice perhaps, considering how closely the character of Monostatos corresponded to the students' idea of the Shah). The demonstration was preceded by a teach-in at the *Freie Universität*, in which the students were instructed about the authoritarian nature of the Shah's rule.

The demonstration took a tragic turn. A student, Benno Ohnesorg, was killed when the police attacked and dispersed the demonstrators. Following the same pattern, the German students' nationwide actions against the establishments of the newspaper and publishing house of Springer were intended to draw attention to the reactionary character of a great monopolistic publishing chain, which had, in the students' opinion, misrepresented their cause. The riot at the Frankfurt Book Fair in September 1968, on the occasion of the presentation of an award to Leopold Senghor, the President of Senegal, and a distinguished French poet and, to the French intellectuals, an apostle of negritude, also had a pedagogic intent: to draw attention to the fact that in Senegal President Senghor had called in paratroopers to restore order among rebelling Senegalese students.

These examples follow the same pattern. They are preceded by a lesson, in which the reasons why the Shah of Iran (or the Springer establishment, or President Senghor) should be attacked are explained to the student demonstrators. The public, who in at least two of these cases must have been completely ignorant of the reasons for the students' indignation

11

against foreign guests to their country, are supposed to deduce the lesson communicated from the mere fact of there being a demonstration. This serves also to show the violence (deliberately, and as a matter of policy, provoked by the students) of the police, in their reprisals.

The French students showed, in their demonstrations, their flair for making a serious point with humour, impertinence and passion at once public and intimately personal. One event among others, which signalised the beginnings of the Movement of 22 March was the raid conducted on the corridors of the girls' dormitories by the boys at Nanterre. This was at once a shocking (to the bourgeois) assertion of the modern students' sexual demands (which are not just that he should have sex, but that doing so should be openly recognised as his right) and a protest against the greyness, the bureaucracy, the lack of personal communication at the new university.

Daniel Cohn-Bendit in his book *Obsolete Communism: the left-wing alternative*[1] insistently links up sex with his ideas about the university and revolution. He traces the origins of the students' movement first to the student protests at Berkeley in 1964, and then to a pamphlet published in collaboration with the review *The Situationist International* by the Strasbourg students in 1966, 'On the poverty of student life considered in its economic, political, psychological, sexual and intellectual aspects and some means of remedying it'. What is important here is that sex is brought into the open on the same level as abstract or social topics, like one stone – and not a concealed one – in an edifice. If it is 'private' then it is a privacy which has to be asserted as a public right, precisely because if this is done it fuses the private with the public. Some critics sneer at the students for their equating what are called in America 'parietal rights' with issues like Vietnam, as though to do so is frivolous. I think these critics are wrong. That the students want to relate intimate personal values of living with public values is one of the most serious aspects of their movement.

After the most important of all issues – Vietnam – the most publicised issue chosen by the Columbia students for protest

[1] Cohn-Bendit's book is published by André Deutsch, 1968.

was the commencement by the administration, in a public park adjoining the campus, of the construction of a gymnasium to be used by Columbia students, and also to be accessible at certain hours to members of the Harlem community, through a basement entrance in the park. The administration was supposed to have been overbearing in its attitude to the community in the plans for this project.

Another issue was the presence on the university of the interest of the IDA (Institute for Defence Analysis) which was involved in research for the war in Vietnam. Columbia University had in fact withdrawn from the IDA, but President Kirk (a special target for the students) remained on the board and this perhaps signified some lingering involvement.

The building of the gymnasium, or rather stopping it being built, seemed an effective issue. It dramatised the relationship of the university authorities with Harlem and called to mind a long history of complaints by the community and of high-handedness by the trustees and administration. It concentrated on the relationship of the blacks with the whites. Moreover, it committed the militant whites firmly to the cause of the blacks: though this subjected them to humiliation when the whites, who had seized Hamilton Hall together with the blacks, were pointedly asked by the blacks to leave. The row about the gymnasium was a reminder that Columbia University is a white enclave in a black area.

Beyond all this there were further problems, characteristic of most great American universities but perhaps worse at Columbia. A president scarcely visible to students and faculty, absorbed in the concerns of American college presidents, fund-raising, dealing with trustees and alumni, administration; a growing administration coping with the problems of dealing with a growing student and faculty population, and producing the impression of a faceless bureaucracy (to use a rebellious cliché); an ever widening gap between students and faculty; and the faculty rather helpless, with no effective influence on university affairs. The role of some members of the faculty as would-be peace-makers during the disturbances, is curious, rather touching. They made, as we shall see, proposals that

13

were liberal and sensible, but in order to carry them through they had not only to negotiate with student leaders, but with the president, alumni, trustees and administration as well.

I have suggested here that the students chose issues which were simple and concrete like those in history books. They are also like history in that the more you look at them the more complicated and questionable they become. Take, for instance, the matter of the gymnasium. When one looks into it, it does not provide an example of overbearing behaviour by the Columbia University authorities, which it is taken to be. It is much more complex than that. The proposal to build the gymnasium goes back to 1958, and at that time it seemed a step towards improving relations between the university and the community. The Cox Commission Report[1] says that in 1958 there was an agreement between the parks commissioners and the president of the university for the university to build a gymnasium in the park which contained facilities for community use, as laid down by the parks commissioner. Thus, although building on an open space which was public property, the university was giving the neighbourhood some extremely useful equipment, for which the university not only paid the expenses, but also $3,000 annual rent.

The attitude of members of the community, and of students, towards the gymnasium underwent a good many changes in the 1960s. Organisations representing the community, and the New York authorities, had different attitudes at different times. The Cox Commission states that serious opposition to the project did not begin until mid-1965. But 'by the spring of 1968, the opposition both in the community and among the faculty and student body was highly emotional, widespread, and deeply rooted. Contrary to statements by Columbia officials, this was – in the context of 1968 – a racial issue'. The question of the gymnasium became politics when it was thrown into the mayoral campaign of autumn 1965. Then 'John Lindsay issued a White Paper on the city's parks which criticised the gymnasium project and called for revaluation'. A new parks commissioner, Thomas Hoving, took sides against it.

After this it is rather surprising to find the writers of the

[1] Cox Commission, *Crisis at Columbia* (*The Cox Commission Report*), New York (Random).

Cox Commission state: 'Although it is hard to recapture the atmosphere, there is little evidence that the gymnasium was an important campus issue prior to the April disturbances. Most people seem to have felt that it was a *fait accompli*.'

Bearing this out, Daniel Bell, Professor of Sociology at Columbia, in an extensive essay on 'Columbia and the New Left',[1] writes that the 'big issue' of the year at Columbia in 1968 was recruiting for the Dow Chemical Company and for the military on campus. There were small protests against the military – 'a pie was thrown' – and the 'Dow Chemical recruiting had come to nothing – only a few students signed up for an interview, then withdrew their names – and the Dow recruiter came and went quietly'. As for the gymnasium, Daniel Bell writes that in a poll made by the Columbia newspaper *The Spectator* it was found that half of the neighbouring Harlem community had never heard of it. Of the remaining half 56 per cent favoured the project.

And when on 23 April there was the historic students' meeting at the Sundial it was not primarily about the gymnasium: but to protest because six students had been put on probation for violating a ban which had been imposed on indoor demonstrations; and to agitate about the connection of Columbia with IDA. The gymnasium was only put on the agenda at the last moment presumably because the black students of SAS (Students' Afro-American Society) had quite recently taken it up as an issue. Cicero Wilson, a black student, made a speech demanding that work on the construction of the gymnasium be immediately stopped. At the end of the meeting a letter was delivered to the demonstrators from Vice-President Truman offering to meet them immediately in McMillin Theatre. They said they would do so only if they were allowed to form there a 'popular tribunal' which would try the six students who were under probation. Vice-President Truman's emissary could not accept these terms without referring them back to the President. Exit. There was then some confused discussion which was followed by the crowd attempting to enter Low Library, and then being diverted to the gymnasium site where they tore down a section of a fence. One of their number was apprehended by the police.

[1] *The Public Interest*, Fall 1968 (no. 13).

So the importance of the gymnasium emerged out of a whole series of actions which were improvised, but which became symbols. The gymnasium had the advantage – from the agitators' point of view – of being under construction. A fence was there, so they tore down part of it. Someone was apprehended so they also apprehended someone – Mr Coleman, the Dean of Columbia College, in Hamilton Hall. The students, white and black, then occupied Hamilton Hall. Later the black students asked the white students to leave; which, dazed and shocked by the request, they did. Then, as they had been turned out of one place, improvising still, they occupied another, Low Hall, and, later on, various other buildings.

On the following day, 24 April, some members of the faculty formed a group called the Ad Hoc Faculty Committee, for the purpose of mediating between the militant students and the various avenging forces which they had conjured up: their fellow students – the so-called 'jocks' – who did not approve of their methods and who wished to throw them out of the occupied buildings, or at any rate to prevent them from receiving supplies; the administration, liable to call in the police and thus create a new situation the results of which it was impossible to foresee; and the police themselves. What the Ad Hoc group most effectively did was to form a kind of special constabulary of volunteers, with ribbon arm bands who kept the hysterical, the vindictive and the authoritarian apart.

I have read several reports by members of this band of guardian angels. They regard their mission as a failure – for the police were called in at the end of the month and behaved with the automatic and predictable savagery which never fails to astonish. I do not think the Ad Hoc volunteers give themselves enough credit for all they did in demonstrating love of their university and good will to those who acted erroneously or reacted too violently. Possibly the tireless watch they kept will be remembered after all the wearisome exaggerated issues which set off the revolt are forgotten by all but the professionals of minutiae. They proved that the spirit of the university was alive and aware. During my visits to the campus I always had the sense of a few spirits surrounding these ugly buildings, like prayer. Once again the liberals deserve two cheers.

The Ad Hoc group made proposals for compromise – that

16

work on the gymnasium should be suspended; that disciplinary power should be vested in a tripartite judiciary body; that strike leaders should not be victimised, but that there should be collective punishment for the demonstrators. The president and administration were evasive and legalistic, the SDS leaders intractable. Finally, on 30 April the president called in the police and the students were evicted, with considerable brutality. The black students in Hamilton Hall, in accordance with arrangements made by the black psychologist, Kenneth Clark, left without fuss.

One night that week I had dinner with the young writer, Frank Conroy. Ivan Morris, whom I had met in Japan, was one of the guests. He argued that the students had acted peremptorily and violently about issues which could have been settled by other means, and some of which – for instance the connection of IDA with the university – were under discussion by the administration. Ivan Morris pointed out – as Raymond Aron was to do about the Sorbonne – that a university is a delicate organisation which can be damaged irretrievably, as had happened with the universities in Japan. Ivan Morris is both genial and severe, rubicund, rather eighteenth-century in appearance and with an energetic manner of expression. His criticisms did not seem to be made out of hostility to the students. So after meeting him, I wrote to Japan for such information as I could get from the English language newspapers there. The reports bore out what Morris had told me. A few weeks later in the London *Times* (2 October 1968) there was a summary of the amazing state of affairs in Japanese universities, which had continued for at least a year, the *Times* correspondent wrote. It is a story of repeated riots, ammunition trains blocked, television programmes dominated by the students, processions of students carrying flags in front of the prime minister's office and American bases. There was a climax to these events at Nipon University when ten thousand students (out of a campus of eighty thousand) compelled the chancellor and five other university directors to promise to resign. In the course of this meeting the chancellor and the five directors 'were forced to bow deeply to the ten thousand students and admit their

17

negligence' – an almost unthinkable humiliation in Japan. As a finishing touch to these proceedings a young police officer was killed by having dropped on him 'a big chunk of brick or concrete dropped from a sixth floor window'.

Ivan Morris has publicly countered the grievance of the students about the gymnasium, with a charge of vandalism. They are responsible, he asserts, for the burning of the manuscript – the work of a lifetime – of Professor Ranum, during their occupation of a building.

Other professors, at first sympathetic to the students' demands, complain that they found that when they tried to meet their terms, the students changed them, making new demands which it was impossible to accept.

The Process of Radicalisation

During the uprising, on one occasion I was asked to go to Columbia and talk to a group of students about universities. I did so, rather autobiographically (I am not an expert and can only speak from my own experience), pointing out that during the Thirties Oxford and Cambridge became centres for anti-Fascist agitation and that, as long as the undergraduates did not break the laws, they met with no difficulties in using the university partly as a political forum. The mistake, I suggested, would have been to destroy the university instead of drawing on it as a place of learning, a library, as Karl Marx used the British Museum. Afterwards, one of the students asked me what I meant by the process of radicalisation. I answered: 'It's what happens if, when you're in a position more or less to the centre, you congenitally feel that those to the left of you are in a more correct position.'

This is what happened to many of the students. As the result of their radical action they found themselves either becoming more radical or persuaded of the correctness of the more radical leaders.

Radicalism, as a continuing process, started from their committing themselves to actions in response to the classical grievances (the gymnasium, the IDA). They soon found that they had further grievances, which pushed them into further action, or into making demands in excess of the original ones.

18

The representative of Columbia at an international meeting of students held at the London School of Economics in the early summer of 1968 made this very clear, without perhaps realising how revealing he was of himself. This lank, loosely knit young man with a lock of black hair falling over his pale forehead, and his appealing eyes, talked about protest against the war in Vietnam, the IDA, the gymnasium, and other student grievances. What he told us, the audience, with evident satisfaction (and with confident anticipation of the approval of his audience) was a tale of improvised action leading to ideological postures. Waving his arms which were spread wide, as though he were conducting the audience, an orchestra, and looking coyly down at them with his boyish conspiratorial drawing-us-all-in-grin, he explained that the capture of Dean Coleman was the reply improvised by *us* in response to that blundering folly of arresting a student committed by *them*. 'We wondered how we should reply, and thought "Let's take a hostage!" so we took the Dean.' *Laughter and applause.* 'We took the Dean, and we were very nice to him.' The argument ran that *our* political convictions are revelations, lightning at the touch of improvised action. We took one building and that made *us* want to take another. We groused about the gym and IDA and then, in a flash, we saw that the whole university was a microcosm of the society which produced these things. Politics meant to the speaker the ideas that resulted from the action by which you put yourself on the spot. He wound up by saying that the university serves the existing power structure. Once you see the truth of this dazzling proposition, then unless you act, you and your ideas are, he culminated, bull-shit.

Everyone did not agree with this view. The German representative, Dr Krippendorf, shook his blond-maned, spectacled head. He even seemed a bit shocked. He said that idea should not spring from action, action should be the result of carefully considered idea, theoretical groundwork. The students should think first and act afterwards, as Russian students had done in 1905. The ideological absoluteness of his thinking was demonstrated by the example he gave of the difficulty of persuading the academic mind to think politically. How difficult it was, he complained, to make a professor teaching eighteenth-century literature understand that in doing so he was helping the cause of the American intervention in Vietnam. What the students should do was to make themselves thinkers who could analyse such matters as the way in which the bourgeois concept of objectivity undermines progress. The students should also avoid having leaders who subscribed to a cult of personality. He recommended practical ways of achieving this – or of avoiding it – such as constantly changing leaders, and forming a pool on which they could draw, of those qualified to lead.

In putting thinking before improvised action, the German SDS are the opposite of the Americans at Columbia. However, from opposite extremes both arrive at the same conclusion, that students should be completely politicised, that all action and behaviour has political significance, and should be criticised as being for or against the revolution.

Looking at things in this way, the American SDS leaders are brought to the conclusion that the university itself fulfils a political function in the society. As Lewis Cole says in an interview published in *Partisan Review*:[1]

One of the questions that has been against us is this: if the university is so interconnected with American society, how could you possibly change its nature unless you changed the nature of the society itself? The answer is that you cannot; but I think perhaps you can have such a thing as a neutral university – that is, a university which, though it doesn't help liberation movements throughout the world, at least does not help counter-insurgency movements.

This slip into finkism is at once corrected by his colleague, Mark Rudd:[2]

I don't think that possible, really. Even if you did away with things like IDA and support for governmental policy, you would still have to look further into the question of funding in the university. Look at Columbia. Columbia makes its money off real estate.

The point is further hammered home when the interviewer challenges Cole and Rudd by quoting at them the remarks of one of their chief authorities, Herbert Marcuse, who did not support their view about the universities:[3]

[1] Lewis Cole was in fact the student speaking at the London School of Economics, where he may have given a wrong impression of himself. At any rate, the account is only my impression. *Partisan Review*, Summer 1968; 'Interviews at Columbia University', by Stephen Donadio.
[2] *ibid.*
[3] *ibid.*

20

I have never suggested [Marcuse said] or advocated or supported destroying the established universities and building new anti-institutions instead. I have always said that no matter how radical the demands of the students, and no matter how justified, they should be pressed within the existing universities and attained within the existing universities. I believe – and that is where (my) finkdom comes in – that American universities, at least quite a few of them, today are still enclaves of relatively critical thought and relatively free thought. So we do not have to think of replacing them by new institutions. But this is one of the very rare cases in which I think you can achieve what you want to achieve within the existing institutions.

Rudd and Cole, with this thrown at them, find a strange inconsistency in Marcuse (who so clearly sees the pervasiveness of conditioning thought in all the other structures of the consumer society) having what Rudd calls 'a blind spot when it comes to the controls and limits on thought in the university, which are tremendous'. Talk of the universities being places of 'relatively' free thought reminds him, he says, of talk about 'a temporary partial bombing halt'.

Radicalisation is a process which hardly permits one to think otherwise. As Mark Rudd points out:[1]

When we started this, we were talking about changing a few things: the gym, IDA, etc. But then people began to talk about student power and a free university and everything else, and it got completely away from us ... And so what we're engaged in, to use a piece of SDS rhetoric, is the process of radicalisation; we make no bones about this.

One consequence of radicalisation is constantly extending your demands against those who are trying to negotiate with you, so that the original demands are lost sight of and replaced by new and unexpected ones. It means using an institution – the university – as the board of a game played by rules which one of the players constantly re-invents, to the disadvantage of the other, and in which buildings, classes, examinations, etc. are pieces of the game.

Quite apart from whether or not the students who embark on this radicalising process wish to wreck the university, or whether they toy with the idea of regarding it as a neutral scene

[1] *ibid.*

21

for political activism, there can be no doubt that if the campus were to consist of the pieces in such a game and there were sufficient students playing it, there would soon be no university. In some Latin American countries the universities have already become scenery, like target sites, for semi-military games between students and police or army. But for the students to wreck the university is self-destruction. Without the university there would be no students. The position of the students, even as agitators, depends on there being the university.

Some of the student leaders seem quite prepared to accept this. Dwight MacDonald summarises the aims of Tom Hayden as follows:[1]

The goal written on the University walls . . . was 'Create two, three, many Columbias' [a reference to the late Che Guevara's 'Create two, three, many Vietnams in Latin America']. . . . Expand the strike so that the US must change or send its troops to occupy American campuses. . . . Not only are these [Columbia] tactics already being duplicated on other campuses, but they are sure to be surpassed by even more militant tactics. In the future it is conceivable that students will threaten destruction of buildings as a deterrent to police attack. Many of the tactics learned can also be applied in smaller hit-and-run operations between strikes: raids on the offices of professors doing weapons research could win substantial support among students while making the university more blatantly repressive. . . . The Columbia students want a new and independent university standing against the mainstream of American society, or they want no university at all. They are, in Fidel Castro's words, 'guerillas in the field of culture'.

As MacDonald points out, the word 'student' is used here with an arrogant disregard for the views of most of the students, since in a poll among students taken at Columbia 'only 19 per cent of the students favoured the tactics of the demonstrators, while 68 per cent were against them'. One may add to this that the idea of acting provocatively in order to make the authorities more obviously repressive is bad tactics because it is so transparent.

The Charter of Nanterre, drawn up by a national convention of

[1] *New York Review of Books*, 22 August, 1968, quoted by Lawrence Stone, chairman of the History Dept at Princeton University.

revolutionary committees of faculties of French universities (at the Sorbonne, 22 June 1968, by 143 votes to 9 with 8 absentees) declares that the student movement 'has assumed its full dimensions by joining the workers' struggle against capitalist society'.[1]

The same programme of using the universities as outposts from which to attack and revolutionise society, provoking the police, is advocated by the German students of the SDS (Sozialistischer Deutscher Studentenbund – Socialist German Student Federation, not to be confused with the American SDS, Students for a Democratic Society).

The students who take this position demand in effect that the universities become the instruments of an Open Conspiracy against the society in which they exist.

Lawrence Stone, chairman of the History Department at Princeton University, sums up the 'Charter of Nanterre' as meaning that 'the function of the university is to work for the subversion of the society which surrounds it'. Declarations of the American and of the German SDS amount to the same thing.

It needs to be pointed out that to say this is equivalent to saying that the university should itself be destroyed. For those who argue that the university should be supported by the society in order to subvert the society, also believe that revolution is necessary precisely because the society would permit the university to do no such thing. Moreover if the university were in fact permitted to be free to the point of its endangering society, they would certainly argue that the apparent freedom of students to attack the society was illusory: for they regard the university as a microcosm of a society which cannot turn against itself.

It is important to have a clear idea about the extent to which the university can be critical of society without the university's own existence being endangered. Here the fact that the student movement is international should be an advantage. For by comparing his position and the possible consequence of his actions with those of students in other countries, the western student should be able to judge better the extent to which he is free to criticise the society without wrecking the university.

[1] *New York Review of Books*, 22 August 1968.

It should be quite clear to him, looking at the Japanese and the South American students, that a university can be wrecked. It should also be clear that in Moscow or Madrid no student could make a statement such as this declaration of a former president of the German SDS:[1]

This movement is radical, anti-authoritarian and anti-capitalist. . . . It refuses to accept the rules of the game of the parliamentary bourgeois democracy whenever these become formalised as administrative instruments for the preservation of the system. The right to demonstrate in the centres of our cities takes priority over traffic regulations and police regulations which aim at forcing the demonstrations into suburbs and empty streets.

Black Tactics

The black students at Columbia were joined in Hamilton Hall by a considerable number of blacks from other colleges, and from the Harlem community, and they were advised by black power leaders. They were also in a position of strength, for the administration never forgot that they had potentially behind them the Harlem community. Diana Trilling declares melodramatically:[2]

Even without the danger of invasion from Harlem, there was sufficient in the Columbia disturbance to suggest a catastrophe in nature, but with Harlem on its borders a measurable catastrophe might have become an immeasurable disaster – the university might be overrun or burned down.

Given their position of strength, the blacks acted not just as if they were black power fanatics who wished to destroy the university and then the society – in that order – but as though they were a foreign power which had a cold but realistic relationship with another power – the university – in which each party, though they were enemies, understood that much might be gained by respecting the other's integrity.

In fact their behaviour was maturer (perhaps because they accepted the advice of older people) and less neurotic than that of the improvising white students.

[1] The quotation by a German SDS leader, Helmut Schauer (past SDS president) is from F. C. Hunnius, 'Student Revolts', *The New Left in West Germany*, p. 31, A War Resisters' International Publication, 5 Caledonian Road, London N 1.
[2] Diana Trilling, 'On the Steps of Low Library', *Commentary*, November 1968.

From a psychological point of view the improvisation of the white students, although it led nearly always to aggressive acts, declarations and postures, was a disguise behind which they allowed decisions to be made for them which arose as the consequence of those acts. Even the famous policy of provocation – provoking the authorities to behave worse than you do in order to 'unmask' them – had something passive about it. For when the authorities had acted as a result of the provocation then those acts determined the reactions of the students. Moreover the policy of provocation – based on the assumption that the police and other authorities always, if attacked, behave worse than their attackers (this is what unmasks them!) had the effect of putting the originators of the provocation in the position of being victims.

'They arrested one of our students. We said we must have a hostage, so we took Dean Coleman.' 'We took this building then we wondered what to do next, so we took another.' At first this looks positive but the more one examines it the more negative it seems. Who decides what? The student leader who talked like this, in each case explains the students' actions as the result of their being acted upon. He went on to explain their policies as the result of the reaction to others' action. Their behaviour arises from a situation in which they have been placed. The fact that sometimes they have placed themselves in the situation makes no difference, because they still explain their behaviour and even their ideas as the result of something that has happened to them. However aggressive they may be, they are always victims.

The row about constructing the gymnasium was of course separate from the various actions and ideas which followed. But the students altered their demands and made them extend far beyond that of abandoning the construction of the gymnasium. The gymnasium triggered off a series of acts and ideas which at the end had little to do with the original issues. These had been left far behind. The process of radicalisation begins with their wanting *not* to build the gymnasium; it ends with some of them acquiescing in the idea of destroying the university.

The same pattern of a kind of negative aggressiveness is to be found in the attitude of the white students towards the members of the faculty with whom the students were negotiating, when they kept on altering their demands. I cannot believe that in doing this they were coldly calculating. They altered their demands because as a result of their improvising which placed them in new situations they discovered that they had new demands. This was the process of radicalisation. I think too that some of them expected the members of the Ad Hoc Committee to 'understand' that as a result of their involvement in 'revolution', the Columbia 'commune', their demands would change together with their ideas. With a side of them which was still childish they were testing members of the faculty who they supposed to be in a parental relation to them: confronting them with the problem of 'understanding' that they, the children, were simply demanding that their elders should see the consistency of attitude and feeling beneath the inconsistency of their altered demands. The statements made by the faculty members show that to some extent they responded to this like parents. They understood. As Lionel Trilling explains:[1]

But it has almost never failed that when I meet the students themselves . . . I find that, contrary to my first expectations, I have great respect for them and that their demands at least begin to make sense. I think that what happens is that when I confront them personally I see them in their cultural and social situation, and since I understand why this should arouse their antagonism and rebelliousness, I am the better able to see why they should direct their protest at the university, which they take to be representative of the society, as the part of the society with which they are most immediately involved and which is most accessible to their protest.

But some of the complaints of the students are surely those of children who, frustrated in the desire to be closer to their parents, aggressively assert their independence. There is an ambivalence about the student demands which leads to paradox. To judge from some statements and programmes put out by the white students, with demands for the 'critical university', for marathon debates among themselves, for 'student power', you might suppose that they never want to see or hear from their professors again. Yet one does not have to look very deep to realise that one of their grievances is that they have too little relationship with their professors and that they feel shut out

[1] Lionel Trilling, *Partisan Review*, September 1968.

26

from the functioning centres of university life. A question I asked at Columbia was why they had chosen to occupy the president's offices. They looked puzzled, then one answered, 'I guess it's because we wanted to know what they look like inside'. I mentioned this to Professor F. W. Dupee, and he observed that he had been teaching at Columbia for twenty-five years without ever realising where the president's offices were.

In an article appearing in *Evergreen* (August 1968) Dotson Rader, a student who took part in the Columbia uprising, shows much of the ambivalence of the rebels towards the older generation. Rader divides the faculty into those who he evidently hopes will take the students' side, and those, like the president and the top officials, who he hopes will be shown up in all their villainy. Lionel Trilling, the great scholar and critic, and liberal, represents those who he hopes will choose the students. Inside the 'liberated' Mathematics building, Rader recalls:

I sat there and wondered where Lionel Trilling was, hoping that somehow he, who wanted to understand so badly what was happening to us, would come over to our side. I remember telling him that in relation to his generation we felt disregarded, unconsulted, power-less – powerless to effect the quality of our lives in his America. Our lives, without roots in history, seemed diminished to gesture, without power, to desperation, without probable hope, to fantasy.

He makes it very clear that he is sitting in the Maths building not because he believes that by doing so he can help change the society but because he has joined his friends in rebelling against the System:

What other choices are there? Trilling's generation had covered all the options. We were left with our resistance and, in this culture, that meant acting in danger to ourselves.

I think that this feeling that a generation old enough to be their parents – grandparents even – 'had covered all the options' is shared by many of the students. The options of one genera-tion become the traps, the choices that cannot possibly be made, for another. They cannot be made partly because they were proved to be wrong. The Thirties chose the wrong kind of revolution, the one that ended with war and Stalin. Nothing is clearer to a later generation than the naivety of an earlier one, just as nothing is clearer to the earlier one than the naivety of the later.

The students feel deserted by the older generation. Dotson Rader recalls their feelings at the time of the march on the Pentagon:

At the Pentagon we waited late into the night – Lowell and MacDonald had parties to attend – in the growing tension and the cold [here I should mention perhaps that after half an hour of Low Library, I had to leave in order to go to a party in New York] . . . waited around fires built on the steps before that massive, ugly building, waiting, hoping in the dark that the troopers' fingers would tighten and bullets would fly and it would be over for us. We wanted to force them to act irrevocably. We wanted a response *to us.* Any kind: and now at Columbia I waited, knowing they could not act affirmatively in regard to us, they could give nothing without endangering the whole fucking System. 'We have to consider,' President Kirk had said, 'what effect our action will have on other American universities.' I wanted them to act as they must, to act against us, to reveal themselves for what they are – a stinking rotten group of venal men, and the others had reached the point where we could no longer tolerate being disregarded. I and the others had to own our lives.

The least the authorities could do was act in a way which proved to the rebels that they were the victims.

The black students, criticising the white students essentially for their lack of maturity, pointed out that the white students regarded themselves 'primarily as members of an academic community', and for this reason went in search of student power. The observation is penetrating. The white students continue to regard the alma mater as theirs, physically part of them almost, like the parents whom children abuse dreadfully but who know that nothing can destroy the fact of parenthood, the tie of flesh. Reading their statements I found myself constantly surprised by the assumption, underlying all the proposals for setting up counter-universities, wrecking the university, that the university would not forsake them. However, and wherever kicked around, it would carry on, face-lifted, in new dress, acquiring all the latest ideas, wishing to please. The picture of the university as a family, perhaps a broken family, holds true of France as well

28

as of America. These dreadful rows and tears, all these long sleepless nights, this talk of spanking and punishment, all hold out the promise of reconciliation – if only the children in their recklessness don't, without realising what they are doing, break up the home.

Both professors and students at Berlin told me that one of the things most wrong in the German university was the traditional distance between the exalted professor and the students with whom he only had dealings through his subservient assistants. When the *Freie Universität* was founded in West Berlin after the war, it was planned as 'a community of teachers and learners', and indeed before it had been moved to its splendid American style campus at Dahlem, and when it was still being conducted in lecture rooms improvised from halls and cinemas, it was this as, participating in one or two discussions there, I was able to see for myself. These good intentions have been swept away, partly as a result of the immense expansion of the university, which made it impossible to select teachers who accepted the principle of participation and partly because the students used their students' parliament to make national politics which were embarrassing to the West German government. But it is noteworthy that the 'Critical University' which the students of ASTA planned in Berlin was in many respects a return to the original aims of the Free University. Instead, though, of there being a teacher-learner relationship, in the Critical University, teachers and learners are regarded as equals almost. Parents and children have become estranged, so let us all be brothers and sisters, lovers, together.

The personal or psychological reasons for rebelliousness of some American students are doubtless connected with that much-discussed subject the 'crisis of identity'. Notoriously the young white American has difficulty in establishing his identity as a *person* in a society which holds up goals of being a good American, succeeding in the rat race of business or political life, by standards which are so largely those of the mass media. To be a student offers promise of some kind of identity, yet many students feel even more lost in the vast spaces of the crowded modern campus than they do at home. To be a

29

rebellious student is an emphatic assertion of identity, especially since what is new and special about the rebellious American students is that, although deeply political, they remain colourful and fantastic, combining often the personality of the hippy with that of the theoretical revolutionary.

Further light is thrown on the problem of identity of the rebellious student today by some observations of Erik H. Erikson in his book *Identity*:[1]

The utopia of our era predicts that man will be one species in one world, with a universal technological identity to replace the illusory pseudo-identities which have divided him and with an international ethics replacing all moral systems of superstition, repression and suppression. In the meantime, ideological systems vie for the distinction of being able to offer not only the most practical, but also the most universally convincing political and private morals to that future world; and universally convincing means, above all, credible in the eyes of youth.

Much of what I say in this book illustrates these remarks. For the rebel students identity means on the one hand an expanding and embracing consciousness of belonging to a world community, and on the other hand their separate identity as individuals or as pairs (hence the insistence on sex as a kind of private flag which you wave before the whole world). In seeking for this expression of an expanding consciousness they are brought up against the offers and promises extended by ideological systems. What is original about their generation is that they look these gift horses in the mouth. They have a particular distrust of current systems and for that reason study past utopias of anarchism which they seek to put into modern dress.

In his book *The Young Radicals*,[2] Kenneth Keniston describes the dilemma of the young American who is in the position of being what he calls a 'latent radical'. He looks at the surrounding society, is appalled by it, and comes to the conclusion that effective action is '(1) essential but (2) impossible'. Obviously, to the socially conscious young, this feeling of impotence, unless it is surmounted, itself creates a problem of identity. Keniston suggests that it is solved either by the

[1] Erik Erikson, *Identity*, London (Faber) 1968.
[2] Kenneth Keniston, *The Young Radicals*, New York (Harcourt, Brace) 1968.

'latent radical' becoming convinced that action might be effective, or that success does not matter. He joins forces with those who immerse themselves in action, he discovers through action that he has revolutionary ideas.

But the black students who occupied Hamilton Hall did not have any doubts about their identity, which was by no means dependent on their student status. Their identity was decided for them, one might say, by their not being white students. They regarded themselves as representatives of the West Harlem ghetto at Columbia.

The Columbia uprising had become primarily the concern of the blacks. The white students had made this be so when they tore up the section of the fence round the excavated site of the gymnasium, and thus based their uprising on the racialism which the gymnasium supposedly symbolised. In these circumstances the black students behaved with great coolness. When the white students seized Hamilton Hall on 23 April, the blacks infiltrated into it and, as we saw, greatly to the dismay of the white students, asked them to leave. They wanted the white students out of the building because the presence of the whites in the same building spoiled the colour confrontation, the drama of us – the blacks – in Hamilton Hall, against them – the whites. The blacks had simple and clear demands: that the construction of the gymnasium be abandoned; that all ties with IDA be severed; that amnesty be granted.

Another reason why they regarded themselves as well rid of the whites was (as they explained to Stephen Donadio, the *Partisan Review* interviewer) because they regarded the whites as vacillating and 'unable to make a clear decision on their role'. They thought the black students had more discipline than the white and were not so given to 'revolutionary rhetoric'. It was clearly understood by those in Hamilton Hall that what was going on was a demonstration, not the revolution.

The white students certainly had reason to be greatly shaken. Their symbol of unity, the controversy over the white-black issue at the projected gymnasium, had turned against them. The blacks were treating them with the same contempt as they treated whites who were not on their side.

The situation is parallel to that of the French students, embracing the cause of the workers, who marched to the Renault factory at Billancourt, which the striking workers had occupied, and were turned away at the gates. But for the French the humiliation was not so great. The Renault works were, after all, proletarian territory, and the young bourgeois from the university approached Billancourt from his own Quartier Latin. The white Columbia students were in the position of being turned out of their own buildings.

It is unthinkable that they, any more than the French students, should reject those who rejected them, as they might well have done if they had been asked to leave by a leftist political party or the leaders of a great trade union. Why? In the answer to this question lies much of the secret of the student movement. It is that in the relationship of the American and French students to the blacks and the workers there lies much more than politics. They bring to this relationship their apology that they are white bourgeois, their regret that they belong to the oppressing race or class, their wish to be forgiven, reconciled, and even loved.

If, in this situation, the blacks reject the whites, they can only respond by saying: 'We deserve to be rejected!' and 'Give us our orders. There has been so much injustice on our side that you are justified in dictating your demands, whatever they are.'

Here present events cast back light on the Thirties. One reason why the bourgeois turned anti-bourgeois found it difficult to criticise the Communists was that they were to him the 'workers'. He brought in consideration of their case a sense of guilt that washed away any sins of the proletariat, just because it was the proletariat.

The relationship of the black students to the university was, as I have said before, that of diplomats who are on the point of breaking off relations with another power, who will resume them if their stringent demands are met, and who do not care whether relations are broken off or not – they are an independent power – but who recognise that there are advantages for both sides in keeping them going.

As Bill Sales, one of the black students interviewed, says:
If the university responds effectively there may be mutual benefit

32

growing out of what happened from April 23 to 29. If the university doesn't respond effectively I'm not really qualified to predict what will happen but I suspect that there will be increasing tension and that it will come to seem that solving problems of this kind through the normal means of discussion and protest is no longer a possibility.[1]

It was the black students who in fact controlled the situation. What the authorities most feared was a racial riot, with black victims, on the campus. They could have put up with white victims far more easily.

The black student representatives observe that the black students viewed themselves as 'an extension of the black community', identifying not with the university, nor with white America: they were just themselves, a foreign country. When, at the end of the month, the administration finally called in the police to clear the seized buildings of students, the black students simply came out quietly, giving themselves up, while the white students carried on their protest. And the black students took no part in the month-long strike of students that followed. The black students made themselves look formidable in the eyes of their white enemies, the administration, and they succeeded in making their allies, the protesting white students, look adolescent.

The white students, as I have said, had a problem of identity which they resolved first by being students, secondly, more emphatically, by being rebellious students. The black students, opposite here as in other respects, had a problem of losing their identity through desegregation. Their identity is, of course, immensely real, in some ways the most real thing in America. This may seem exaggerated. Yet the very strength and might of white America is of a vast, depersonalised, depersonalising force, in power, industry, advertising, propaganda. Many of the most personal things in American life come from the Negro culture, jazz, and the Negro influence in southern literature, which makes it so remarkably distinct from all other American writing.

The identity of the blacks does not in the least depend on their being students at white universities. On the contrary, the blacks are waking up to a realisation that desegregation is a

[1] Bill Sales, *Partisan Review*, August 1968.

threat to their culture. They are beginning to ask themselves whether the aim of the planners of the Great Society is not that the blacks should end up finding themselves middle-class American citizens, with the standards of the shopping centre.

Two fantasies arising from the situation at Columbia University, throwing events into grotesque light and shades, are worth recording.

During these events a plot occurred to me which seemed close to the sick humour of American musicals. I imagined a musical called *The Last Liberal*. During a strike on a great American campus, the blacks seize a building, as at Columbia they seized Hamilton Hall. A liberal professor – white – joins them, and is received with enthusiasm. All contact with the world outside is cut off, and there is nothing to eat. After several days all supplies run out. The liberal professor has to offer himself to be eaten. He does so. There is a party.

I told this to a black friend of mine. He said: 'Well, I have a plot too. It is that the Great Society opens training camps all over the United States, into which blacks are invited. There they will learn, they are told, to be middle-class American citizens. They accept gratefully. They are taught English accents, how to behave at high-class shopping centres, what are the right things to buy, and so on. Then one day they discover that the training camps are concentration camps, and they are all going to be put in hygienic gas chambers.'

So if the neurosis of the white students is the fear that they have no identity, the passionate search to find one, that of the blacks is fear that they will lose theirs, and beyond this the fear of actual extinction. This takes extreme forms, as in the demand – like that made by black students at North Western University – for black colleges on white campuses with nothing but education in black history and culture taught by black teachers. That the black students should reject desegregation, and demand instead a new kind of segregation, but on their terms, is a shock for the whole society like that of the white students when the blacks asked them to leave Hamilton Hall.

Worst of all, however, is the reaction which may be the result of the students' uprising. One day I drove with Lionel and

Diana Trilling from downtown New York up to Columbia. When we said 'to Columbia University', the taxi driver started telling us what he would do to the students if he had his way. What the police already had done, and even what on 30 April they were to do, did not at all exceed the taxi driver's sadistic fantasies. I was soon to find that taxi drivers in Paris (when they were not on strike) and in Berlin shared much the same view of the students. The taxi drivers are representative of the vast number of middle-class Americans, as was shown at the time of the Democratic Convention in August, when the great majority of Americans, even after they had seen the full horror of the brutalising of young Americans by the police, showed that they backed the methods of Mayor Daley.

Strategy is something to which the students have scarcely paid attention. Yet in some respects they are God's gift to the strategy of the other side. What the taxi driver's reaction shows is that they are regarded with envy by great numbers of an older generation, who have not had adequate education, and who secretly think that given advantages of school and university they could have become professors or presidents of corporations. Students who revolt seem, to these middle-class masses, to be throwing their advantages back in the faces of those – the middle class – who pay for them. The one cry to which all presidential candidates in America had to pay attention above all others in the election was the demand for law and order.

Notes on the
Sorbonne Revolution

The Barricades

The street battles which took place near the Sorbonne in mid-May between students and police were ritualistic. In the late afternoon, while it was still daylight, the students started building barricades. Those I saw on Friday (24 May) were particularly elaborate. First they tore up paving stones and piled them up as though they were rebuilding memories of 1789, 1848, 1870. Then, in a mood of dedicated desecration, they axed down, so that they fell lengthwise across the street, a few of the sappy plane trees, spring-leafed, just awake from winter. Then they scattered over the paving stones and among the leaves, boxes, wood, trash from the uncollected strike-bound garbage on the sidewalks. Lastly, as the night closed in, they tugged, pulled with much rumbling, neighbouring parked cars, braked but dragged over the streets just the same, and placed them on their sides, like trophies of smashed automobiles by the sculptor César, on top of the paving stones, among the branches. In an arrangement of this kind on the Boulevard Saint-Germain, they had extended the contour of a burned-out car by adding to it the quarter section of one of those wrought-iron grills which encircle at the base the trunks of trees on the boulevards to protect their roots. After the night's fighting, this chassis had acquired a wonderful coral tint. On its pediment of bluish paving stones it looked like an enshrined museum object. It was left there for two or three days and much photographed by the tourists who poured into the Quartier Latin during the daytime.

There was not a sign of a policeman while the barricades were being built. Presumably the rules of what has become a war game were being observed. Within a few days the police, after having attempted to occupy the Sorbonne and the university district early in May, abandoned the territory of the Sorbonne.

The Boulevard Saint-Michel was student territory. The students controlled the traffic. They did so with extraordinary pride as though their square mile of Paris was an independent republic. However the completion of the barricades was the sign that the territory may be invaded. The police are now to be let out of the long crate-like camions with thick wire netting over the windows behind which they wait like mastiffs. One sees them assembled at the end of the boulevard near the bridge. Their massed forms in the shadows, solid, stirring, helmeted, some of them carrying shields, seem those of medieval knights. A few of the students also carry shields, the lids of dust-bins, and swords or spear-length sticks. Slowly the massed police advance up the street like a thick wedge of mercury up a glass tube. The students retreat to their barricades and set the trash and wood alight. The police now start firing tear gas shells and detonators which make heavy explosions. When they are within a few feet of the advancing black mass of police the students run away, occasionally picking up and hurling back shells which have not exploded.

The Beatnik word 'cat' suddenly occurred to me. The wild, quickly running, backward and sideways turning, yowling and scratching students were like cats, the police stolidly, massively pursuing them were like dogs.

Terrible things happened to students who were caught and taken to the police cells.

A friend, the painter Jean Hélion, told me of a couple seen weeping over the burned-out cadaver of their car on which they had spent their savings.

The Sorbonne

The centre of the Sorbonne is a courtyard enclosed by cliffs of buff-coloured stucco walls. They don't shut out the sky but at the top they make an ugly edge against its flat oblong. There are two tiers of rather grandiose steps across the whole width of one end of the courtyard leading up to the pillared chapel. Along the sides of the courtyard there are now tables piled with books, magazines, pamphlets, leaflets, etc., all of them 'revolutionary'. Behind the tables students sit, displaying these wares.

NOTES ON THE SORBONNE REVOLUTION

Most of the slogans and posters appear to proclaim Communism. But a closer inspection reveals that there is no variety of Communism here to offer any comfort to Moscow or the French official Communist Party. Even a magazine called *La Nouvelle Humanité* turns out to be Trotskyist, abhorrent to the sellers of the old *Humanité* who have been banished to the outer gates at the entrance of the building. The brands of revolution offered by the students are Maoist, Castroite, Trotskyist. Pictures of Mao, Che Guevera, Trotsky, Lenin, Marx, are displayed on walls, hoardings, pamphlets, and leaflets. Stalin's portrait put in a brief appearance but quickly disappeared.

One day there was a table for Kurds, Turks, Arabs, and Algerians; posters attacking Zionism were on the wall behind them. That too disappeared. The Sorbonne is cosmopolitan French culture. Among the bewildering assortment of advertisements, appeals, bulletins posted everywhere or leaflets thrust into your hand, I noticed directives to Greek, Spanish, Portuguese, and German students, some of them written in their own language. And of course there were Americans. Two sat rather insecurely at a table collecting signatures for a petition in support of Mendès-France. A committee of American students hangs out at the sister offices of the Sorbonne in the Rue Censier. Here too are the American draft-resisters. They seem lonely, dejected. They ask me what means they could use for getting publicity for their cause. They give me copies of a stenographed news sheet which they circulate.

The Censier is full of classrooms, lecture rooms, offices on every floor. One floor seemed to consist of a nursery. There was a classroom of poets who sat at a table with sheets of paper in front of them, writing poems, presumably. One of them comes over and shows me a poem he has written which consists of mysterious hieroglyphs. He explains to me that these have a prophetic significance, denoting the end of the world. The poets have gone rather far in decorating their rooms with way-out paintings. A lady comes in and asks whether anyone has a pot of paint, as there have been protests about the obscenities on the walls.

Entrances lead out of the Sorbonne courtyard on to passages and stairways, all of them plastered with notices. Almost every departmental office and classroom has been taken over by committees, organisers, planners, talkers; Committee of Action, Committee of Coordination, Committee of Occupation, Committee of Cultural Agitation, and the sinisterly named Committee of Rapid Intervention, the Katangas.

There seems a tendency for the movement to proliferate cells, activities, categories, subdivisions. I noticed that the Commando Poétique has its functions subdivided into: '*Tracts poétiques – affiches poétiques – création collective – publications à bon marché – liaisons interartistiques – Recherches théoriques – commandos poétiques révolutionnaires – praxis poétique révolutionnaire*'.

The poems I saw (*Le Monde* published a selection from them) seemed a mixture of surrealism with the socially conscious leftist writings of the Thirties, and a return to the political style of Eluard. The real poetry of the revolution is its elegance, politically revolutionary, but imaginative and witty. The poems more revealing of the deepest impulses of the movement than most of the pamphlets and pronouncements. They all come together – as do all the finest impulses of the students – in the magnificent summary: 'Imagination is Revolution'. One understands from the slogans why the students cannot get on with the great trade unions, political parties, official communism:

Prenez vos désirs pour des réalités.
Monolithiquement bête, le Gaullisme est l'inversion de la vie.
Ne pas changer d'employeur, changer l'emploi de la vie.
Vive la communication! A bas la télécommunication.
Plus je fais l'amour plus je fais la révolution, plus je fais la révolution plus je fais l'amour.
Luttez dans la perspective d'une vie passionante.
Toute vue des choses qui n'est pas étrange est fausse.

Some slogans offensive in a personal way to the general and the police had a way of appearing for a few hours and then disappearing, perhaps to put in a momentary appearance again. There was one which appeared after a night when some students had been badly beaten up by the police, which I found touching in its appeal. It appeared once, I was not able to find it again. '*Flic, méfis-toi des stimulants qu'on met dans ta soupe.*'

After General de Gaulle's return from his state visit to Rumania on 18 May, he was reported to have made his famous comment on the disorders which he found in France: '*La réforme, oui; le chienlit, non.*' There was wide speculation on the meaning of the guardroom term *chienlit* (*chie en lit*); after a good deal of debate in the Press it suddenly became accepted as meaning 'mess-in-the-bed'. The students marched the streets shouting in their remarkably enunciated rhythmic chorus:

> *c'est lui lui*
> *le chie-en-lit.*

Notices started to be chalked on the walls referring to the state of the general's sphincters. They quickly disappeared.

The Explosion of Talk

In a classroom at the Sorbonne there is a discussion going on about the nature of work in the consumer society. The room is crowded and contains older as well as young people. The discussion is dominated by two young men, one of whom, in the well of the classroom, is evidently a worker. He has a lean face with jutting features and bristly, straw-coloured hair emphasising the line of the back of his head which seems almost continuous with his neck. He talks about work, which, he says, in all circumstances must be hard and boring. The opposite of work, he says, is pleasure, and he describes, quite exhibitionistically, his own holidays which are spent, it seems, in driving about the country on his motorcycle and laying as many girls as he can. Obviously this is the opposite of what is meant by work.

He is confronted by a student standing a few feet above him. He is small and dark and vigorous and has in his eyes and on his lips an expression like that of the blind made miraculously to see in a cartoon of Raphael. He says that work is joy if you are one of a group, a collective (any backward echoes of that remark are suppressed by his smile), joy is participation, it is release from the self. He describes holidays that he and his companions have made together where they have done a great deal of work. The individual must not be like the bourgeois intellectual, alienated and separate, existing in no 'social context' but that of other intellectuals like himself; nor must he be a cog in a machine. He must be in society like a fish in the water. ('We are in socialism like fish in water,' a Czech student said to me in Prague in July.)

43

The worker interrupts and says, You are not talking about work, you are talking about sport. Sport is not work, it is the free development of the individual. Work means taking orders from someone set above you. The student says that in the revolution, automation will replace the kind of work which is slavery. Work will then consist of participation. There will be no oppression of power because there will be a constant to-ing and fro-ing between those at the base of society and those at the top, a vital current. Machines will function but the goods and services they produce will be a means for leading a life of better value, and not ends which prove that the individual owns things or acquires status. He says the students and the workers combining together could achieve this kind of society: not the intellectuals who are void because they reflect problems peculiar to them, outside the context of society. To be truly revolutionary, you have to experience reality.

This discussion was naive. Often at the Sorbonne and the Odéon one heard worse than naive, talk that was chaotic and stupid and dull, and one longed to hear a professor talk for half an hour about Racine. There was wisdom though, perhaps, in talking simply as an act, like action painting. Talk, uninhibited, crude, theoretical, confessional, has overtaken Paris, Lyons, Bordeaux, and other cities. It is the breaking out of expression long suppressed. Not just the Sorbonne and the Censier, the Beaux Arts, the Odéon, were filled with talk but also the streets themselves. Another part of the French revolutionary tradition has emerged – the idea of joining forces with others in the streets – *dans la rue*!

In the Rue de Rennes I find myself standing in a group of shoppers and shop assistants outside a closed Monoprix. A frustrated shopper is saying indignantly, 'Where will all this end? In Communism, universal poverty.' 'Not at all,' says a natty, black-coated worker, 'Communism means *more* refrigerators, *more* television sets, *more* automobiles. *Le communisme, c'est le luxe pour tous.*'

This definition shows how difficult it is for the students – conscious, many of them, of themselves as bourgeois, and seeking for a world in which material things are subservient to other human values – to get on with the workers, most of whom, of course, want consumer goods. The relation of the French

44

students to '*les ouvriers*' is a love affair in which the guilt-conscious bourgeois are trying to win the members of what they regard as a wronged class to their own values.

They equate revolution with spontaneity, participation, communication, imagination, love, youth. Relations between the students and young workers who share – or who are converted to – these values are of the first importance. They dramatise a struggle not so much between proletarian and capitalist materialism as between forces of life and the dead oppressive weight of the bourgeoisie. They are against the consumer society, paternalism, bureaucracy, impersonal party progress, and static party hierarchies. Revolution must not become ossified. It is *la révolution permanente*.

Not that the students want altogether to dispense with washing machines and refrigerators. Their attitude is shown in a document of thirty theses drafted at the Censier by a group called *Les Yeux Crevés*. It begins by defining the students as a privileged class, not so much economically as because 'we alone have the time and possibility to become aware of our own conditions and the condition of society. Abolish this privilege and act so that everyone may become privileged.' It goes on to say that students are workers like everyone else. They are not parasites, economic minors. They do not condemn '*en bloc*' the consumer society. 'One has to consume, but let us consume what we have decided to produce. . . . We wish to control not only the means of production but also those of consumption – to have a real choice and not a theoretic one.'

What is poignant is the gestures of refusal. Again and again I have the feeling that the students' is a world surrounded by traps, past and present. Bourgeois traps, Communist traps, traps set for them by the older generation, but traps also into which members of that generation, seeking to avoid traps, fell. Hence:

Students, refuse 'revolutionism'. It isn't a question of making a revolution, never mind what revolution, because it won't make itself. REVOLUTION IS NEITHER A LUXURY NOR AN ART. IT IS A HISTORIC NECESSITY WHEN EVERY OTHER WAY IS IMPOSSIBLE.

Students, refuse categorically the ideology of 'output' [*rendement*], of 'progress' and such-called pseudo-forces.

Students, do not give way to the blackmail of apoliticism. Our struggle has always been political and can only be so. Refuse the palliatives of understanding, paternalism and common sense which are asked of us.

Against a world whose remedies and palliatives they reject:

Students, count on our youth, our immaturity, to make it happen that everyone has a free choice, and can become truly adult, mature, responsible.

Students, refuse the deaf dialogues of words, but refuse also the dialogue of brutal and conventional force. KEEP THE INITIATIVE. DON'T LET US DIG OURSELVES IN BEHIND FIXED POINTS NOR BEHIND BARRICADES. DON'T LET US BE ON THE DEFENSIVE. LET US ATTACK!

One thing – perhaps the only one – which the Paris students have in common with the Beatniks and Hippies of the psychedelic generation is that they wish to live the life of the revolution even while they are taking action to bring it about. But they are opposed to drugs and similar eccentrically individualistic forms of self-realisation; partly because their view of the revolution is of a community rather than of the individual, but still more because they have a sharp awareness of the counter-revolutionary effects of drug taking.

Yet one should not write the Beatnik influence off. Their long hair, their uncared for yet picturesque dress, the masculinity which includes the feminine and does not go in for any he-man Hemingway cult, all this is Beatnik. Although at any moment everything might turn into the political struggle, ideological interpretation, discipline, it has not done so yet. When the chairmen say 'un peu de discipline', they mean a very little, just that little without which we shall be able to accomplish nothing. Occasionally Beatnik texts spring from the walls: La propreté est le luxe des pauvres, soyez sales.

The students are reluctant to discuss the Bolsheviks and the anarchists of the Spanish Republic who also said they wanted direct democracy. Or, reminded of this, they take refuge in the idea that theirs is an unprecedented generation. To recall the failures of previous revolutions is to seem in their eyes patronising, paternalistic. The London Times in an editorial pointed out as a weakness of the students that they did not appear to have read George Orwell's Animal Farm. But they would not want to

46

read it and if they did read it could find there nothing which they thought applied to their case.

It is significant that the movement of the students at the Sorbonne – called the movement of the *22 Mars* – started among sociologists at the newly built extension of the university in the desolate industrial suburb of Nanterre. A long declaration by Cohn-Bendit and some of his colleagues, in *Esprit* (the May number), depicts the sociology students as seeing sociology as a statistical account of existing society, the result of American influence. The very few sociology students who would get jobs after they left the university would be engaged in such activities as making consumer reports. Sociology instead of being an instrument of bourgeois society, could be turned against it to make a revolution and construct a new society. Sociology today plays in their mind the role of philosophy in the Communist manifesto. Instead of being a passive study it becomes the society lived and willed, but society directed against existing capitalist society. Here the beginnings of an ideology of the students are implicit.

Inevitably, perhaps, the students are un-selfcritical. They do not notice inconsistencies in their own attitudes, even when, to an outsider, it must seem that these could be disastrous. This struck me when I heard a student who had organised the revolt at Strasbourg University describe his experiences to a great gathering in the amphitheatre of the Sorbonne. He spoke about the professors with whom the students had to deal with that kind of contempt which is current among some students. He told how he had been asked by someone why he had not explained things adequately to the authorities at his university, and how he had answered: 'because one does not enter into discussions with people who are nonexistent'. People you do not talk to because they are nonexistent! Whatever justification there might be for adopting this attitude when confronted with the stuffed geese of Strasbourg, I could not help wondering as I listened how it would work out in the 'direct democracy'. Supposing – I thought – our student from Strasbourg goes to a factory or to a village where there are peasants, is it not likely that he will meet a few people with attitudes not altogether dissimilar from those he encountered at Strasbourg – people 'who understood nothing' (*qui n'ont rien compris*) (that was another of his phrases for describing those who did not agree with him)? And had not one heard all this before? Did not the Soviets start off very willing to talk to anyone and everyone who agreed with them, and then make the horrible discovery that there were still bourgeois elements floating around, that there were recalcitrant peasants, people who understood nothing, people finally whom one stops talking to – or just stops talking. At this point the phrase '*On ne parle pas avec des gens qui n'existent pas*' begins to acquire a sinister ring.

The students are, I emphasise, conscious of these dangers and do not wish to repeat them. Yet I wonder what might happen if someone wrote on the walls of the Sorbonne: 'The streets of Hell are paved with good intentions.' If it were written there, I wonder how long it would last. I noticed that they are very good at deleting.

The students perhaps because they are so insulated in the Sorbonne, as though on a stage set, keep reminding me of behaviour and characters in literature. There is something about their movements which reminds me of *The Lord of the Flies*, with a thuggish Katanga 'Committee of Sudden Intervention' ready to emerge from the cellars to produce a final fall. When one has stepped into the Sorbonne one often seems to be in the world of *Alice Through the Looking Glass* where all the values of the circumambient trafficking world outside are reversed.

J-P Sartre at the Sorbonne

On the evening of 20 May at 7.20 p.m. I went to the Grande Amphithéâtre at the Sorbonne to make sure that I would be in time for the grand spectacular of the writers, '*les écrivains*', at which Jean-Paul Sartre was due to appear. It was announced for 10 p.m., but already the vast hall was so full that I only just managed to squeeze myself in between two French students and an American girl with snub nose and button eyes in a square astonished face. At about 8.30 Mary McCarthy and Mulisch, the Dutch writer, appeared and took seats reserved for the Press of which there was a single row all the width of the platform at the back, right under the endless mural of Puvis de Chavannes. I managed to extract myself from my human sandwich and by climbing a barrier to get on to the platform, where I took a chair next to Mary McCarthy. After a space of ten minutes which was filled by various student and worker speakers making orations of which no one took the slightest notice, members of the vast audience in the area in front of the platform, and in the several galleries which went up to its roof, started shouting in chorus demanding that those seated on '*la scène*' should remove themselves. The chairman or chairmen, for there were several student leaders by now trying to control the crowd, shouted back that these places were reserved for the Press. As I was not the Press, I told Mary that I would sit among the crowd of people along the side of the platform. Feeling cowardly, I did this. Rather to my surprise someone politely brought chairs for us: the other two had now joined me. We felt happier, strategically speaking, being not quite so directly in the line of the immensely concentrated fire of this public; though through being on the platform at all we were still exposed to vociferous criticism from the audience who evidently felt that they exercised some kind of right to arrange the grouping of the personnel on the platform. Sitting there looking at that immense shouting, moving, gesticulating mass was like looking into a cavernous mouth full of raging teeth. Or, to put it differently, one's position on the platform, moveable, seemingly, at the concentrated will of this public, was like that of iron filings on a sheet of glass under which there is a powerful and impetuous magnet. They would certainly have provided a lesson to any theatre producer studying how to produce a chorus, for they were capable of reciting with multitudinous incisiveness not just the terrible hissing phrase '*assis!*' but whole sentences like 'Away with the photographers!' and '*Nous ne voulons pas des personnalités!*' or, to individual speakers, 'We don't want to hear you!' From what might be called the bridge of the platform, behind the long table where the chairmen were gesticulating, the audience must have looked like a stormy sea these unfortunate pilots were trying to weather. The pilots called out despairingly '*pas de désordre!*' and '*un peu de discipline!*', both of them phrases which involved them in a surrender of principle (one felt the anguish in their voices) or taught them a terrible lesson – since this audience was surely an irreproachable model of spontaneity and revolutionary manners.

49

And all the time, quite inexorably, the hall went on filling until one imagined – one could not *not* imagine – its sides bulging, like leather or a concertina. All the gangways were blocked to suffocation, figures clung in clusters to the ornaments of balustrades between the galleries. To cheers, a girl managed to worm her way into a niche high up on the wall, and seat herself on the knees of a statue of PASCAL, to be followed soon by another who stood beside her in the niche.

Somehow in the midst of all this turmoil M. Max Pol Fouchet, a director of French television, manged to make a speech in which he courageously declared that he and his colleagues were fighting for freedom of televising. He concluded with a gesture that took me thirty years back to Madrid, a clenched fist, to a not altogether responsive audience. His jutting jaw seemed to be trying to imitate his fist. Then one of the chairmen managed to command sufficient silence to be heard saying that the hall was so full that it was impossible for M. Sartre and the *écrivains* to reach the platform. Howls. Execrations. But it was clear that the chairman bore the audience no malice. He was merely calling their attention to a physical condition. For now the chairmen at their table seemed merely clinging to a raft. The dense opaque sea of the audience had filled in from every side. There was – one realised – no interstice through which J-P Sartre could penetrate. Nevertheless, the chairman went on, M. Sartre had consented to come. It seemed a miracle, for sure enough, there was Sartre by the table, looking at the audience through his spectacles with lenses thick as portholes, and all the waves and winds were hushed. Sartre immediately started explaining that this was not what he had expected. He had not come there for a public spectacle, a literary event. He had come to enter into dialogue, by question and answer with the students. He proposed therefore that the audience should disperse and reassemble in adjoining halls and classrooms to one of which each of his literary colleagues and himself would go. . . . Asking this was like asking the audience to become a sea anemone and achieve parturition by bisecting itself. They did not want his 'chers collègues'. They wanted him in spite of their contempt for personalities, in spite of the fact that they had refused to listen to Aragon, sent by the Communist Party, like a lion tamer, to soothe and smooth them, in spite of the fact that they had

rejected Françoise Sagan with one of their best choric achievements I was told – 'Get back to your whisky and your boy
friends' (or was it 'your Mercedes'?); they wanted to hear
Sartre. They might have added that it was unfair of him to
complain that he was not there as part of a literary spectacle –
for it was exactly as such that the posters had announced the
meeting – and that it is even more unreasonable to complain to
an audience that it is too large than to complain to a fat man
that he is too fat.

Finally Sartre resigned himself to answering questions, and
in some extraordinary way the audience did succeed in turning
itself into a spiritual entity like an attentive small group!
Questions were asked and Sartre, computer-like, produced
small neat packaged answers in his crackling voice. This had a
little tin added to it by the loud speaker from which it emerged
somewhere behind several hundred people in the wall behind me.
The transformation of the meeting into an attentive seminar
was a warm recognition of Sartre's best qualities, his integrity,
his inability to compromise, his warmth. It was also the
realisation of a great virtue in the audience that they were able
to transform themselves – to recognise, to listen, to become
bored even (they started thinning out), instead of remaining
intoxicated on their self-excitement.

I found myself unable to listen to much, thinking about
Sartre. It seemed to me that he has a warm heart and a cold
brain. The warm heart acts as a boiler which drives the human
engine so that it arrives at the Sorbonne in real response to the
students. But having got there, the cold brain takes over and
produces the answers of sliced logic. All the same the humanity
gets through.

Crabbed Age and Youth Cannot Live Together

One evening, as I left the Odéon theatre, two youths, looking
more like Dickensian street urchins perhaps than students,
called to each other: 'Why doesn't he cut his hair?' 'Perhaps he
should cut it with his nails!' 'Perhaps it's a wig!' Respect for
white hairs was certainly not one of the dues paid in Paris that
May.

51

Usually, though, the old just feel invisible as the blacks were supposed to do in America. 'The young make love, the old obscene gestures', a slogan in the anarchist magazine *L'Enragé* runs. They have read *Romeo and Juliet* it seems, but not *Antony and Cleopatra*.

I observed to a contemporary that I enjoyed, on the whole, my invisibility. He said: 'I thought that too until I went one day with my twenty-year-old son to the Sorbonne. I sat there quietly, and as I had to slip out early was specially gratified to be a ghost. But directly I had gone another student came up and said to my son: "*Qui était ce vieux con avec toi?*"'

One night I was at the Odéon, Jean-Louis Barrault's old-style *avant garde* theatre which the students had 'liberated' and made open for completely unplanned marathon discussions which went on almost till daybreak. The scene was like the sixth act of some play in the Theatre of Cruelty in which the audience had rung down the curtain and taken over the house for their own performance. And they found themselves much more entertaining than Ionesco and Beckett, I am afraid. The performance itself – the debates for which there are no subjects set – could be chaotic, and I was often sorry for the student chairmen who stood in the aisle yelling '*Silence! N'interrompez pas! Un peu d'ordre! Discipline!*'

Everyone called everyone 'comrade'. Here we were in the world where the revolution had already happened, although there were also intruding misbelievers, generously admitted, howled at, but nevertheless, despite many interruptions, intermittently, fragmentarily, listened to, because whatever might happen later (and I had these fears), the students were most scrupulous in their attempt to be open to all points of view – even that of Gaullists and of the Fascist members of the '*Occident*'.

On a particular occasion I was suddenly struck with a thought – a hysterical gripe – that I ought to communicate to the Sorbonne students the fact that when I spoke with the students at Columbia some of them had asked me whether the students at the Sorbonne had any thoughts about them. I was no emissary, I had not been told to say anything and yet I felt I should transmit this. So, comforting myself that with my white hair I would not be listened to anyway, I touched the arm of the particularly vigorous young man who was conducting the audience and gradually acquiring some of the mannerisms of Leonard Bernstein, and I mentioned, humbly, that I would like to say a word. There was only one disapprobating yell (which was silenced by the young chairman with a severe *'On a écouté même Jean-Louis Barrault, pourquoi pas lui?'*) and I started to speak my poor French to what seemed an electric silence. To my amazement they listened and then started asking questions. Could I compare the situation of students in American universities with that in France? One student even offered the opinion that the American students were far more advanced than 'ours'. Then someone asked whether it was true that all American students were always under the influence of drugs. I struggled to answer these questions and then, at the first opportunity, left the theatre and walked to a bar. I was followed there by three students. One of them came up to me very shyly and said: *'Monsieur . . . Monsieur . . . Est-ce que c'est vrai que vous êtes M. Marcuse?'*

When the discussions at the Odéon happened to light on a 'subject' they could be serious and very sympathetic. One night a young man got up in the gallery (people spoke from whatever part of the theatre they happened to be sitting in) and (with his head, seen by me foreshortened from below, seeming to butt against André Masson's patchwork-coloured ceiling) he stated very simply that he had taken into his care some adolescent delinquents. He felt he was having little success in helping them, and he would like to hear the views of the audience about delinquency. At this speaker after speaker got up and discussed the problem, seriously, sensibly, though without saying anything original.

It was surprising how many people there turned out to be social workers. The conditions in prisons and slums that they reported were deplorable. The discussion continued on a level of concern and without silliness for over an hour. After which I got up to leave, but was stopped at the exit by a Tunisian student who said to me: 'They all talk about the harm prison does people – but to me it did good. I was sent to prison in Tunis. I cried, I cursed, I kicked them and I was beaten, and I prayed all day, but at the end of two years I started writing poems and stories, and for that reason here I am – thanks to prison – at the Sorbonne.' 'Go and tell them that,' I said and followed him back into the theatre where, a few minutes later, he made his speech, which, in the telling, turned out to be mostly an attack on President Bourguiba. Still he made his point and ended dramatically: 'From prison, I learned that in order to achieve anything in this life you have to suffer. . . .' A remark which offered none of those present any handle to catch on to.

At this meeting there was a distinguished German lady philosopher, with whom I went out afterward for a coffee. She punctured euphoria. What she noticed, she said, in these discussions, was that they consisted of people saying things as though for the first time, things which had no continuity with anything said before or to be said after. Moreover what was said came out of ideas we had all read in books anyway, ideas snatched from the intellectual atmosphere. She said she thought the real problem was not that the young wanted to have no contact with the old but that, precisely, they lacked contact with truly adult minds. The teachers and older people with whom they had to deal were in fact mentally adolescent. She attributed a good many of the students' attitudes to a shallow nihilism which had been the fashion for a long while. She wondered whether the university had not already been destroyed, and whether it would recover. A university was to her mind not a place where there were only the best teachers but where there were values so pervasive that even an inferior teacher could fit in without letting the standard down.

Postscript and Anti-climax

That May, at the Sorbonne, for a few weeks, the students lived the communal life of sharing conditions, of arriving at decisions by the method of 'direct democracy' – that is to say by consulting the action committees of the movement (*les bases*) and not by imposing decisions from the top – of having meetings which were as far as possible spontaneous, with a different

54

chairman for each meeting, resisting the 'cult of personality'.

However, by the end of May, under pressure from government and police, attacked by the Communists and without support from the *Confédération Générale* of workers, the students had to reconsider their concept of organisation. This they could not do without questioning 'direct democracy'. A Press conference at the Sorbonne on the first of June developed into a disagreement between Cohn-Bendit and the other student leaders as to whether organisation for action and self-defence should arise spontaneously from discussion at *les bases* or should be imposed by the leaders. Cohn-Bendit thought that the dynamism of the movement should continue to come from the *bases*. He is reported in the ill-typed transcript which the Press office issued, as saying:

The only chance of creating revolutionary forms that will not become ossified [*scélérosé*] lies in waiting until a common purpose has been discovered among all the committees of action from discussing matters at *les bases*.

His colleagues agreed on 'spontaneity' as a principle but did not think that the circumstances left them much time for discussion in action committees. They pointed out that they had to decide on measures for '*auto-défense*' immediately. One of them, Weber, said that the committees were too disorganised and uncoordinated to be capable of *auto-défense* in the face of the very well organised Gaullist forces.

The discussion about organisation is crucial, because the danger inherent in too little organisation is defeat by the Gaullist and Communist forces outside the movement; while the danger of too much organisation is defeat by loss of spontaneity from below. The demonstrations and marches, the barricades, were extraordinary examples of spontaneity with a minimum of organisation. The undirected discussions at the Odéon theatre, in which the chairman has to struggle with a tumultuous audience, succeed but do result in disorder and waste of energy. The same must be true, I suspect, of the committees of action. But I sympathise with Cohn-Bendit's view that organisation should not be imposed from above.

During the first half of May a good many Parisian intellectuals, as well as many students, seemed to think of the student revolt as part of a larger revolution which had already happened in France. It was not that. The realisation that the university revolt was threatened added urgency to the debate about 'organisation and direct democracy'.

Journalism inevitably falsifies by concentrating on the scene and the subject, in a situation where what is most significant may be not the scene and not the subject. More important probably than the happenings which I have been describing in Paris in the spring were the non-happenings. Walk a few hundred yards away from one area of the Quartier Latin and despite the strikes and the students there was a remarkably normal atmosphere. One way of describing it would be to say that it was like an over-long, rather restrained holiday, with well-dressed people strolling on the sidewalks, the cafés crowded, the food in restaurants up to its usual standard, and many small shops open. Most foreign tourists, it is true, had gone away, but then Parisians, having nothing else to do, were touring their own city, including the Sorbonne in which the actors were inextricably mixed up with the spectators. The only people who seemed to be notably suffering from shortages (of their clientèle) were the male tarts. I asked one of them what he thought of '*les étudiants*' and he shrieked, with an extraordinary gesture – '*Scandaleux!*'

Dust and dirt from ungathered rubbish exhaled a vague smog, a halo over the streets like old varnish over a new green painting, but the presence of these odours was largely compensated for by the absence of petrol. One had to walk long distances but this was good for health and not much slower than going by car when there is traffic.

The spring itself reasserted what was so much more apparent than the revolutionary situation – the non-revolutionary one. In fact, if there were going to be a revolution, it would happen – everyone I think, agreed – against the evidence of one's senses which lay down certain external rules for revolution. The weather, of course, can be contradictory, but it is difficult to think of a revolution taking place when – in daylight at all events – everyone looks particularly good humoured. For the result of the explosion of talk in Paris this May was that most people looked more self-complacent – even friendly – than they have done in Paris for years.

Yet there was that ugly evening which happened after de Gaulle's second speech in which he adroitly substituted for the referendum he had so mistakenly offered in his first speech a referendum under a more resounding name – a general election. He accompanied this gesture with the release of a flood of gasoline upon which came floating in their automobiles a flood of Gaullists. They came joyously claxoning up the boulevards, hooting at one another, hooting to urge others to hoot, stopping their cars suddenly, getting out to embrace some fellow driver or passenger, in their chic clothes and their make-up, their tawdry elegance, the triumphant bacchanal of the Social World of Conspicuous Consumption, shameless, crowing, and more vulgar than any crowd I have seen on Broadway or in Chicago. It would have been agonising at the best of times, but it was more so when one thought of the students, the self-confined secular monastics of the Sorbonne.

The next day the students had a great parade on the Boulevard Montparnasse and it seemed like a farewell. I walked away from it down the Rue de Rennes and saw an extraordinary sight. In the hot sun, the whole road seemed covered with snow. Actually it was torn-up newspapers. I asked a bystander what had happened. 'Nothing,' she said, 'except that France is mad.' The students had seen announcements in *France Soir* of the end of the strikes, the end of their movement, and they had scattered hundreds of copies of the newspaper, in fury, all over the road. Oddly enough, with all the fighting and the barricades, it was the first sign I had seen of real anger.

If it were possible to speak to them, I would like to say two things. The first is that however much the university needs a revolution, and the society needs a revolution, it would be disastrous for them not to keep the two revolutions apart in their minds and their acts. For the university, even if it does not conform to their wishes, is an arsenal from which they can draw the arms which can change society. To say, 'I won't have a university until society has a revolution', is as though Karl Marx were to say 'I won't go to the reading room of the British Museum until it has a revolution'.

The second thing is that although the young today do have reasons for distrusting the older generation, anything that is worth doing involves their having to get old. What they are now is not so important as what they will be ten years from now. And if ten years from now they have become their own idea of what it is to be old, then what they are fighting for now will have come to nothing.

Czechoslovakia
and Western Students

Bourgeois Freedom – Communist Freedom

For the westerner to go from the west – New York, Paris, West Berlin and London – to the east – Warsaw, East Berlin or Prague – gives him a far more vivid impression of moving from one world to another than to go, say, to the far east. For to the westerner the far east is expectedly foreign, a spectacle seen through bifocal glasses, one half of which shows the tourist paradise, the other half, in sometimes terrible glimpses, the unapproachable, utterly remote reality. But in the People's Democracies the impression is of many different forces moving within diffused general greyness. It is like a canvas portraying a topographical scene of great variety, which has been covered over with layer on layer of varnish which makes one see everything through a monotonous yellow sameness.

Thus Prague is still there, remarkably undamaged in fact. There is the castle, the Charles Bridge, the Hradcany Hill and the palace like an inner city, all the narrow zig-zagging streets of the old town, the buff-coloured walls and the wonderful green light of parks and gardens. All this however seems to have very little connection with the present. It is true that benumbed-looking peasants, bedazzled workers, pour out of buses to look at the national relics. They mingle with tourists who look like dressed up symbols of the currencies they represent, the money they bring in which is – from the government's point of view – the sole reason why they are there.

The past has become simply an object of display like the crown jewels: floodlit caskets behind a plate glass window. The thick fog in which everyone moves is the overwhelming present. Everyone is caught up in the moment of Now. The future offers nothing but the continuance of Now. That is what makes eastern Europe different, I think, from Russia. For despite the weighted gloom of Russia, there is a feeling that behind the oppressiveness, there is, or there was, something serious,

61

something which it is still possible to think made Stalinism better than Hitlerism, the idea that Russia at the beginning of its revolution did hitch its wagon to a future which has never become completely lost. I write this at a moment of very great discouragement, but it is still possible to believe that Russian Communism is merely overgrown by its enormous bureaucracy which has now become the central power, but that at some moment it will cast off this husk and Communism will be capable of a new start in the hands of men who have new ideas and who dare take the risks of greater freedoms.

The leaders in Russia, dismal as they appear, are at least their own authorities, or directly responsible to a central committee. The leaders in eastern Europe have the look of traffic cops, guiding the traffic as best they can through the fog, and communicating with their walky-talkies to the real authorities above. The Ulbrichts, Kadars and Gomulkas are kept there by the dull sense of their unwilling supporters that, subject to the confusion all round them and the pressure from above, they are doing their best. They had better not try any harder: the fate of the Hungarians and the Czechs stands as a warning to leaders who try to lead.

The fog in which the eastern Europeans move is due perhaps to the fact that Communism came when a great deal of its light had already expired. I don't mean that there was not a system, theories, methods and ideas. But there had been Stalin. What had gone – or what burned very low in the old-style Communists who took power too late for themselves and for everyone else – was faith. Without faith there is no past and no future either. There is only an endless continuation of the present, more of the same as before, and a fear on the part of the bureaucrats, who are the guardians of the changeless present, lest things may change.

At the same time, cut off from the past and without a future, condemned to live in the unchanging present tense of Exigency without Faith (and with Hope condemned to deliver all her squeezed-out gains to the Soviet Union), within the dull conformity, people look for freedom, and a few, perhaps escapist pleasures. The underground life of *Rat* emerges from the sewers of the world and sniffs the putrid air of wine cellars and bars, utters some words in its language of the unspeakable,

62

plays a pop song on a guitar. One cheer for *Rat*. This happens in Warsaw and Budapest and even in Moscow. The anti-American America of Greenwich Village, San Francisco and Old Town Chicago is the great international American success.

But much more had happened in Prague this spring than that the underground life had surfaced. The mood was more Apollonian than Dionysian. That is to say people wanted freedom in order to discuss ideas and to take up positions which were not those of the authorities or consistent with party ideology. They wanted to be intelligent. They wanted to reopen the question of the recent past when thousands of people had been imprisoned for political offences. They wanted to discuss how it might be possible to make genuine choices between alternative policies and politicians under a Communist system. They wanted, as they said, to humanise socialism.

Being a realistic people, with heads for business and an appreciation for the useful commodities which make life easier and more efficient, they also wanted more freedom to criticise the way in which the economy was run.

When people in eastern Europe start to talk the language of the western democracies, westerners often react with suspicion. They point out that most countries of eastern Europe have never had democracy. They admit that Czechoslovakia is an exception, but nevertheless they think that slavonic peoples are not really democratic in the way that the English and Americans are, with their two party systems. Since they associate intellectual freedom with parliamentary democracy, they assume also that as far as eastern Europeans are concerned freedom is a kind of luxury for which they have no need as they have never had our 'real democracy'.

In my opinion, this view overlooks some important things. One is that intellectuals, writers, artists and teachers can have a concept of freedom which is independent of a parliamentary system: though they may be strongly drawn to democracy as the best means of realising and defending that freedom. Another is that these categories of people enjoy a freedom in the west which is the envy of eastern Europeans quite apart from the systems of government under which westerners live. A further point is that when people in the east of Europe think of themselves as Europeans, they think that they belong to a commonwealth of tradition and intellect which is not Mr Brehznev's commonwealth of the Warsaw Pact, but whose capitals are Paris, London and Rome. This view is perfectly consistent with their intense pride in their own nationalities. For to them, the nation is part of this Europe. People in Prague, Budapest, Vienna, Bucharest, feel superior to the continent that lies to the east of them; but they do not feel superior to the capitals to the west. They feel their civilisation adds lustre to the west.

Lastly, and most importantly, we do ourselves and them wrong when we despise our freedoms. To all intents and purposes intellectuals and lovers of freedom in eastern Europe, including Russia, mean, when they talk of freedom, western freedom. This is not because it is western but because it is to them, simply freedom, the only freedom they can envisage. This demonstrates that they disassociate the idea of freedom from particular forms of government. It is oversubtle thinking to suppose that when Russian intellectuals like Sinyavsky, Daniel, Litvinov and others say that they want freedom, they mean anything except that they want the freedom which we have in the west, and which they can quite well imagine having under an enlightened and nonbureaucratic form of Communist government. The Czechoslovaks were sincere in wanting to combine the utmost freedom of the individual (by which they meant, precisely, *our* freedom) with Communist government.

It is sometimes said that what we mean in the west by freedom is 'bourgeois freedom' which we generously concede to be a special delusion attaching to our form of society; and that freedom in the context of a Communist society would be, if it is not already, something quite different. Those French and West German students who fail to see any value in the kind of freedoms which are exercised in western universities, say this also. It is therefore important to point out that those who are struggling for freedom in Russia and the People's Democracies mean by freedom very much the freedom that we have. They even talk as though there really was something called freedom that could be taken out of one social context and put in another. Some of the Czech students believed that in the context of the humanised socialism for which they were struggling it would flourish more than under capitalism.

This attitude is shown in an article by a Czech student leader, Jan Kavan.[1] He writes that in March 1968 an assembly of twenty thousand young people approved a declaration entitled 'The Manifesto of Prague Youth'. The first sentence in this manifesto is 'Socialism in our country is a reality'. What the students wanted was for socialism to be 'really enlightened, humanitarian and democratic', and based on acceptance of the United Nations 'Declaration of Human Rights'. From this they go on to claim the democratic right to join with the working people in 'controlling but not overthrowing' their government. In order to do this they ask for 'the provision of legal guarantees of democracy'. Kavan goes on to say:

For us, the classic civil liberties assume the utmost importance. In a socialist society, freedom of speech, freedom of the press, freedom of assembly and freedom of association are essential if the people are to exercise any control at all.

And he adds, very significantly:

I have often been told by my friends in western Europe that we are only fighting for bourgeois-democratic freedoms. But somehow I cannot seem to distinguish between capitalist freedoms and socialist freedoms. What I recognise are basic human freedoms.

Russian intellectuals who are struggling against their government in order to have greater freedom have expressed themselves in very much the same language. The idea that there is a fundamental difference between the kind of freedom that intellectuals wish for in the Communist countries and have in the west, is exaggerated. It is the same freedom.

The struggle of the Czechs is in fact a struggle of a classical kind against authoritarianism, dogma, over-centralisation and bureaucracy. It rests on the proposition that ideas, imagination and simple truth cannot survive in an atmosphere of rigid political and ideological orthodoxy supported by the machinery of the police.

Freedom is not something to be talked about as though it were an abstraction, or a luxury added to a society after it has everything else, the icing sugar on the cake of the economy. In

[1] In *Ramparts*, September 1968.

fact having freedom or not having it qualifies the whole experience of living. It would be a good thing if it were discussed more as something positively consumed like air or food, something the lack of which leaves a terrible void in life, and less as the intellectuals' luxury or the philosophers' theory.

Light More Electricity

As with the American, French and German students, one event signified the meaning of their movement for the Czech students. This was the student march through the streets in October 1967 in protest when the electricity had broken down for the umpteenth time at their students' hostel in Strahov, a district of Prague. For nearly a year, it seems, the lights had failed nearly every night. In addition to the violence used against them, the students were shocked by the way in which the incident was reported in the Press. Accordingly they circulated in typescript their own account of it. This is quoted by Jan Kavan (from whose own writing I quoted above), in an essay entitled 'David and Goliath', which appeared originally in the magazine *Student*, in Prague.[1] It begins:

On 31.10.67 at about 20.30 hours in Anreal [the student dormitories of the Strahov district] the lights again went out. As had happened on previous occasions there was a great deal of shouting from all the housing blocks.

(A plenary session of an organisation called KRAS – The Academic Council of Student Dwellings – happened to be taking place at the time, to discuss the intolerable conditions in which the students were living.) The report continues:

On account of the primitive action of the students the participants terminated their proceeding at 23.15 hours.
Students came out of some of the houses carrying candles in their hands and formed a procession round the reverberating square. This group, whom other students kept on joining, marched a few times round the whole square. Then the crowd of about a thousand went in the direction of Dlabacov. They kept on calling out: 'We

[1] The German version of this essay from which I have here made this rough translation is in *Kursbuch 13*, Frankfurt (Suhrkamp) 1968.

want light! We want light!' The procession passed through the Uvoz into Neruda street. Somewhere halfway up Neruda street a police car passed unhindered in the direction of Porhorelec. The students went on unceasingly crying 'We want light! We want to study!' Entering the upper part of the Kleinstädter Ring the crowd was stopped by the police. The students then tried to get to the lower part of the Kleinstädter Ring, through Neruda street. Here the street was barricaded by police cars. . . . Meanwhile more police cars arrived and energetically began to disperse the crowd. The crowd of students was by now so dense that the students in the front row had no possibility of retreat, and therefore tried to hold back the oncoming police cars with their hands. The police then started using their clubs. When the crowd began to separate the police pursued them in their cars. They attacked those students who did not get away quickly enough with clubs and tear gas bombs, through the windows of their cars. Police who were on foot followed the cars and chased the students. Some, as they beat them with their clubs, shouted: 'There's your light!' According to people living in the district the students went on shouting: 'We want light! We want to study!'

That when the Czech students asked for light they meant electricity, and that when they wanted electricity they wanted it so as to study, and that when the police attacked them the injustice of this was manifest to many more students than those who took part in the procession, portrays in miniature the pattern of the events in Czechoslovakia.

That they struck with their bare hands the cars that drove against them and that the dull functionaries leaned out of their machines and clubbed them shouting 'There's your light!' prophesies the dark postscript of 21 August, with the students beating with their hands against Russian tanks.

Looking back on July when I was in Prague, I think of the Czech students emerging from darkness into the day at which they were still gazing with some astonishment when the darkness closed in on them again. Meeting them in cafés, in the rooms of the Writers' Union, at the offices of the famous review *Literární Listy*, I think of them sitting at tables, or standing in the street, staring straight in front of them, while quietly and confidently they described their situation to me.

The story they told was of the growing dissatisfaction of the more critical minded members of the university with the governmental organisation for Czechoslovak Youth (CSM). This organisation was set up in 1948 when the Communist revolution was still in its euphoric stage, and it seems to have commanded support at first. But later on it became simply the youth branch of the centralised party bureaucracy transmitting the orders and propaganda of the party. The students and faculty of Charles University began to grow critical of it already in the late Fifties. One of the students suggested to me that quite apart from their contempt for the CSM organisation and its leaders there was the affronted pride of a great and proud and ancient academy, Charles University. The students and faculty wanted their own organisation and not to be merged into the national one.

Demonstrations corresponding to those in western universities occurred at the *Mayales* or May celebrations. These were partly students' rags. Once at the *Mayales* there was a jazz orchestra. On another occasion Allen Ginsberg was crowned King of the May. These events annoyed the authorities, and the police. The students came to realise that any unorthodox demonstration led to persecution and expulsions.

Resistance to the CSM and to the party showed in the emergence of various organisations in the university. These were discussion groups and clubs, not overtly political, where students, with the tacit approval of the faculty, expressed independent views. There was TAK, a club for tourism, and SAKS, the students' academic club, consisting mostly of students of mechanical engineering. At TAK there were discussions about Vietnam and the Third World – Communist student subjects – but they were independent of the views of the stodgy CSM. In effect these clubs became pressure groups within the university.

The discontented students were not only those with literary interests. One of the most independent faculties was that of Technical and Nuclear Physics, where there were many active and radical students and also teachers in sympathy with them. Here there were intelligent students and up-to-date young teachers who had not been corrupted by the events that took place in the Fifties at the time of the terrible trials.

The Faculty of Philosophy was among the first where there were people with independent tendencies. By 1963 it became a centre of what were called 'oppositional elements'.

The tactics of the students were to try to set up their own groups and committees, and their own journals, while at the same time demanding that the CSM should be reformed. These demands reached a climax at the National Conference of Students, held in Prague in December 1965, when Jiri Müller, the student leader, demanded radical changes in the structure of the CSM. He proposed that it should form a 'federation' of sections grouped according to social occupation and age. The CSM should itself become the coordinating body for these groups. Müller suggested that as a coordinating body the CSM should be autonomous and independent of the party. He even went so far as to propose that it should be not exactly an opposition but what he called a 'corrective' body to the Communist Party. In a speech at this conference he said: 'The CSM must express and enforce the real opinions of the young people about the methods adopted by the party to achieve its aims. If it is necessary the CSM ought to oppose the policies of the party.'

The students were sometimes mischievous. For example, the group of friends who came to be known as the 'Prague Radicals' had a ploy which they called 'shock tactics'. Through one of the clubs they would invite a leader of the CSM or even from the party organisation to address them. They would then torment him with questions designed to show up his stupidity and ignorance.

The party authorities responded to the demands of the students for independence with expulsions, and by sending the leaders into military service. Thus Jiri Müller was expelled from the university and sent into the army. This happened also to other leaders.

One result of the nation-wide organisation of all Czechoslovak youth was that the students were thrown together with the young workers. The party tried to use the young workers against the Prague Radicals, just as later on they tried to use the workers in the factories against the movement of reform which was started by the intellectuals whom they accused of 'betraying the revolution'. But the Prague students succeeded in winning many of the young workers to their side.

The liberalising movement began among the writers with a conference on Kafka's works which was held by members of the Academy of Learning in Prague in 1963. One of the initiators of this conference, Dr Kusác, told me of this meeting at which Professor Goldstücker – who became in consequence one of the heroes of the liberals – Ernst Fischer and Roger Garaudy were among the principal speakers. Dr Kusác said that strange as it may seem, Kafka was not very well known in Czechoslovakia. He wrote, of course, in German, and was little read up to the war, after which his works were banned. So the Kafka conference was a revelation. This is scarcely surprising since some of his immensely complex stories read like prophecies of the centralised authoritarian police state whose actions and motives are often so difficult to disentangle. One might almost say that in works like *The Penal Settlement* Kafka's insight or prophecy is so literally true that to read it is like looking into too bright a light, so that we interpret what is reality as allegory or myth.

The conference led to the rehabilitation of Kafka, and to a general attack on the censorship. During the conference a question of central importance for Communists was also raised: whether there can be 'alienation' – which Marx supposed to be the result of the environment created by capitalism – under socialist rule, or whether (it is difficult not to report this conversation in the pig German in which Dr Kusác and I conversed) *Sozialismus die Entfremdung liquidiert* – socialism liquidates alienation. Needless to say, the official speakers who were representative of the DDR (the German People's Republic) did not feel in the least alienated, they were perfectly contented inhabitants of their particular sty. Many of the Czech writers took the view that under their experience of socialism with dictatorship and a centralised bureaucracy they had felt alienated indeed. For these reasons, in this Kafka-ish debate, Kafka seemed important: Kafka, whom the speakers from East Germany considered 'dangerous' to socialism.

Dr Kusác told me this while we sat outside a pleasant restaurant, looking out over a public garden: in the dusk, beyond dense green walls, an ochre-coloured wall made a line along one side of a square. Leading downhill there was a street of houses which looked as if they were moulded in plaster. Memories of how Prague looked keep flashing across my

70

attempts to reconstruct conversations. For instance, near the offices of *Literární Listy*, the river, with a view across it, above trees, of the spike-towered castle, Kafka's castle, and the Charles Bridge, leading to the oldest part of the town, on which I was to meet Prague's Hippies.

At *Literární Listy* I met two of the student leaders. They showed me with pride the document *Two Thousand Words*, signed by people prominent in every walk of Czechoslovak life asking that the government press forward with the policy of liberalisation and drawing attention to areas in which it was too slow. That day the censorship had been entirely abolished. One had the feeling of quite irresistible pressure urging these people forward. A man walked through the office with its desks and papers, the usual paper and wooden piled-up crammed condition of an editorial office. They told me that he was the author of *Two Thousand Words*.

But when we talked they were modest about the role of the students in the liberalising movement. They said that they had acted in defence of their positions as students, and not aggressively. It was the censorship, bureaucracy, centralisation and sheer boredom with the CSM which had finally brought them to the position where they found they were criticising the regime. There arose among the students even of the most varied opinions what they described as 'an immense negative unity'. In the end they found themselves obeying what they could only call their conscience.

Then when students were expelled from the university ('in our country if someone is expelled from the university, he carries this punishment to his death') and the police attacked them they began to feel that the methods of the whole society against the students were, as they said, 'unrighteous'. They found themselves in a world where everything became simple. Problems reduced themselves to the question of whether or not they had the courage to do what they knew to be right and to face the consequences. 'There was a kind of tolerance in us for anyone who did not have that courage.'

One of them said of the French students: 'They want to remodel the whole society according to patterns of the inner life, but in doing this they neglect the material means which are needed in order that one may enjoy an inner life.'

When I was in Prague, B——, one of the student leaders, gave me a typewritten copy of an essay he had written. This throws a good deal of light on the attitude of the Czech to the western students. B—— begins by remarking that their western colleagues sometimes reproach the Czech students for not giving more support to the agitation of their colleagues in the west. B—— says he will not go into the politics of this but confine himself to its psychological aspect. 'The fact is,' he writes, 'that the attitude of the Czech to the western students is largely coloured by envy.' The conditions which the western students take for granted appear to the Czech students a dream of bliss. This is why so many of them are ambitious to obtain grants in order to study abroad. He thinks that the western students are so satiated with democracy that they have become fed up with it. They regard it as too formal and as operating too slickly.

Czechoslovak students, he observes rather bitterly, would have been happy if, up till January 1968, they could have lived under such 'formal democracy'. The inspiration which the western students draw from ideas of revolution reminds the Czechoslovak students of their recent experiences.

B—— goes on to remark that the reaction of the younger generation against the old in Prague takes a different form from that in Paris and New York. In the west the students react against their parents being bourgeois, in Prague they react against a generation who had their dreams of revolution. Here he indulges a somewhat strained metaphor. Parents in the east as in the west, both had their dreams of a promised land, and in both places the children have reacted against the vision of the fathers. He does not mean by this however, he emphasises, that the sons of Czechoslovak fathers hanker after the promised land of the west. Nevertheless the intolerant radicalism of some of the western students acts more as a warning than an appeal to Czech students. The Czechoslovak students do however feel sympathy for students when they are brutally attacked by the police as they are in many parts of the world. In any case discussion with western students – and he cites those that took place in Prague with Rudi Dutschke – shows that ideological differences are often only matters of terminology. Their western colleagues lay stress on aims and objectives, whereas the Czechs tend to emphasise the means which should be used to achieve them. They had had bitter experience of how human and lofty ends can be discredited by inhuman means in the period when, in their country, the ends justified the means.

There is a certain papering over of cracks in this, for I do not believe that the meeting of the Prague student leaders with Rudi Dutschke resulted in any real understanding. What is important is the emphasis on ends and means and the Czech experience of the means of the revolution having become the ends. The Czechs give not only the feeling of here and now but also of having lived through terrible realities.

At the back of the Czechoslovak experience there is the memory of the political trials of Slansky and others in the early Fifties. Something of what this means is conveyed in a statement in a newspaper paragraph (*Daily Telegraph*, 23 July) by the then minister of justice, Dr Bohuslav Kucera, that 'between sixty thousand and seventy thousand Czechs, mostly victims of political trials held from 1950 until 1965, and former camp inmates would be rehabilitated under a ten-year programme'.

When I was in Prague in July I met, after several years, a friend of mine, Jiri Mucha, a distinguished Czech writer and son of the *art nouveau* painter Alfons Mucha. During the war, Jiri was a lieutenant, one of the Czechs attached to the Free French. Handsome, gay, courageous, he fought on several fronts of the war against Hitler. He returned to Prague after the war and was arrested in 1951 in connection with the trial of Slansky. To have been attached to the Free French was suffi-cient reason at that time for any Czech to be arrested. He spent one year in solitary confinement being interrogated and con-ditioned so as to give evidence in the trial of men with whom he was supposed to have plotted but most of whom he had never met. He was then sentenced to five years forced labour, spent one year in the coal mines and another year in uranium mines. He wrote a diary now published under the title *Living and Partly Living*, about his year working in the coal mines.

Meeting Jiri Mucha after all these years, there was the double shock of learning what he had been through and of realising that I had not known. I suppose that nearly everyone, without believing in telepathy, has a vague feeling that his friends have become part of his own consciousness. It seems natural that one's thoughts should be with them if they undergo a period of prolonged illness or unhappiness. It seems against nature that this should not be so. But if one is denied this awareness because a government has deliberately kept all knowledge of someone undergoing a terrible sentence from those who love him, it is not only unnatural but wicked. It struck me for the first time that the publication of a sentence of punishment contains in it an element of mercy, however cruel the sentence: because it means that the person punished can be received into the charity of his friends. The secret punishments inflicted by tyrannical regimes are doubly cruel because, apart from the punishment, they make someone non-existent to those who know him. The dictatorship had turned someone vivid and brilliant into a kind of living darkness. They had, as I came to realise, partly succeeded, for there was no thought of what he was suffering in the minds of his friends. When I returned to London one of the first things I did was to call our friends and ask – had they known what had happened to Jiri Mucha? They replied that until his release no one had known.

Most of the students I met were activists – this is why I sought them out. However there was one I met to whom I had brought a letter of introduction. He was a friend of a friend. Since we have re-entered that miserable era when one hardly dares to call people by their real names, let me call him Milan.

I invited Milan to luncheon at one of those small well-scrubbed, panelled restaurants of which there are several in Prague. One shares a table with whomever happens already to be there. Milan was shy. I explained that I was in Prague to inquire about students. I asked him various questions and he gave me a clear, punctilious account of what had happened. He talked in a restrained way as though he saw me on the far side of the gulf across which I looked back at him. His face was, I thought, provincial-Gothic, with high cheekbones that seemed carved from smooth stone, light blue eyes in which the black pupils seemed very precisely drilled by an instrument.

Across the gulf his eyes from time to time looked straight into mine, rather painfully. Then suddenly he exclaimed: 'I shouldn't really be talking to you about this. I am a bit outside it all. I try to lead a private life and to get on with my studies.' He told me that he had a small house in the country to which he went whenever he could and spent his time fixing it up. He was also going to get a dog, and he showed me a book about training dogs which he had with him. In fact, I think he had several dog books. He added apologetically: 'I am afraid that the majority of us Czech students are a bit lazy and indifferent to what is going on.'

After lunch I asked him to accompany me to the offices of an editor whom I interviewed. The editor was helpful, and told me all I wanted to know and mentioned the names of writers. When we had left, Milan said: 'I don't really care about people like that who pay so much attention to writers as though they were gods.' He left me with this, and I wondered whether he disliked me. I wrote then to thank him, and hoped for a reply. I received one in a few days' time. He said that he had had an impulse to run after me when I left and to continue our conversation.

This has a sequel. On 21 August I was working in a remote part of Provence. All that day I felt disturbed about Czechoslovakia. Wanting to do something, I wrote a partly flippant postcard to Milan, which ended: 'How's your house? How's your dog? How's Mr Dubcek?' That evening friends arrived and told me of the Russian invasion of Czechoslovakia. I thought, among many other things, of my card to Milan which at the best might, when he received it, seem callous and mocking, at the worst get him into trouble. A few days later I received a reply thanking me for my card, and continuing:

What can gentle man do against brutality? Do you think that spirit and thought will some day triumph over the physical strength? I firmly hope that Dubcek's ideas are not dead though he was kept like a murderer and sent to Moscow like a luggage. I'm proud anyway that I'm Czech maybe just because of that I am witness of the tragedy of my nation. My personal life is still peaceful.

Strong and gentle was how Prague seemed that summer. One day, between interviews, I walked across the Charles Bridge to the old city. On the bridge there were the hippies in

75

their Red Indian gear, with their long hair and their chains from which hung medallions. They had the odd look of some out-door meeting of a progressive school, for under instructions from someone who looked like a Beatnik schoolmistress, they were laboriously copying out in chalk on the pavement, from copy books, anti-war slogans to do with Vietnam, which they spelled VEITNIM. One of the texts of this ritualistic language (a strange backhanded compliment to America) ran: MOR I AQCUINT MY DOG LESS I LIK MY MAN. Meaning had become ritual in a language in which America was translated into flowers. I borrowed a piece of chalk from them and corrected the English of the slogans. They looked on wide-eyed, and then one of them handed me the notebook asking me to write in it a slogan for them to copy. I could not resist writing: *'The better I know my dog the more I love man.'*

The Czech students were not revolutionaries in the sense of the students of the American SDS and the German SDS and of the movement of 22 March. They had no desire to destroy their universities. They had no quarrel with the older generation and little desire that the young should lead. On the contrary, they considered themselves students by virtue of studying at the university. Their ambition was for the university to be an autonomous body which could possibly become a 'corrective' to the party within the Communist state. Instead of considering the university a microcosm of the society, they considered it as a club or pressure group within the society. They had no quarrel with 'the consumer society'. On the contrary, if it were possible to join it by filling in a form, most Czech students, and I have no doubt, most Czechs, would do so.

A disagreement between West Germans, Americans and French with the Czechs about the consumer society is trivial anyway. It is the haves telling the have-nots that they should not covet what the haves have. When I was in Prague in July, I was told that to buy a car in Czechoslovakia you have to put half of what it costs in a bank and then wait for three years, at the end of which you pay the second half, and, if you are lucky, get your car. If, during the interval, you run short of cash and draw on the money you have set aside, then you are back at scratch and have to start all over again. Families go without meals in order to save up for a car.

So on the level of conditions created by their situation the Czech students were the opposite of those in the west.

If one were asked to sum up in a word the expression on the faces of the students in different countries, one would say of the Americans 'hysterical' (driven to it), of the French 'romantic', of the West Germans 'theoretic' – but of the Czechs one would say 'modest'. They had at once the modesty and determination of their clear and limited aims. There is a danger here though of using the modest demands of the Czech students as a stick with which to beat the western students. It is important then to remember that the Czech students are not confronted with the problem of western students which arise with having guaranteed freedoms, consumer goods, etc. As one of them said to me when we talked about this: 'Maybe we would make the same complaints as the American and French students if we lived in their society, but we don't do so.'

For the western students to blame their Czechoslovak colleagues for being bourgeois (because they want those things which the French students offer up as burnt sacrifice on barricades) and for the Czech students to envy their French and American colleagues for having them is stupid. The mistake in all the chatter about the consumer goods society is to discuss these objects as values in themselves. Once you have got to the stage of relating them to the values of living, then you can, however, discuss whether they add to or subtract from these. Like freedom they can be discussed as benefits experienced or not experienced, capable of use or abuse. This is exactly where there could be a real discussion between students from different countries: for the Czech students have the (now tragic) advantage of their experience, from which their western colleagues might well have much to learn. They have been through the euphoria of the revolution and the black night of fear which followed it. They understand very well the processes by which a revolution may turn into the very things the western students are rebelling against: centralised authoritarian government, bureaucracy, censorship, boredom. Their ideas as to whether these ills can be avoided are worth listening to, though they might, it is true, seem discouraging to the French and

American students. Having very few consumer goods, they have shrewd ideas as to how far these can contribute to freedom and self-realisation, and how far experience in modern conditions is diminished for many people for the lack of them.

Like others who were in Prague during the summer of 1968, I was struck by a mood shared by everyone I met which, looking back on it, seems the most extraordinary I have ever encountered. It was not like the euphoria following the revolution which was that of Barcelona at the beginning of the Spanish Civil War. Still less was it the mood of poetic rebellion of May and June in Paris, with that wild upsurge of all the themes of the past orchestrated to the surrealism of the present. It was rather prosaic, and could give meaning to the phrase 'quiet confidence' were it not so much more passionate than that.

One thing the students shared with their French and American colleagues was sleeplessness and the talk without arrest. What the mood suggested above all was that every thinking person in Prague was being carried forward by invisible forces. And these forces were not yet, as one thinks such impulses have to be, hysterical, irrational and revolutionary, they were rational and sensible. They combined in the most powerful force of all, a sense of absolute rightness. People had to express themselves as they had to breathe. The force was that of people struggling for light and air.

Although concerned with things that were in no way unrestrained, perhaps the fusion of demands, supported by indisputable reason and good sense, was itself too powerful. Here an element of unreason did enter in. People thought that because their demands were so reasonable they must also be irresistible. Under the positive forward-surging currents there was certainly a nervous unceasing current of fear. Some of my friends would ask me what I thought the Russians would do. I replied that what worried me was the thought that they could do anything they liked: there was nothing to stop them. My friends would answer this by saying they wouldn't dare to. By this – with Russian tanks roaming the countryside, the troops which refused to leave on manoeuvres a few miles away – they meant that the Russians would not dare to act so massively and with such exposed obscuranticism against light and reason, with no excuse except their bare-faced power. Besides, I was assured, the Czechs were the only people of the People's Democracies who liked the Russians. At which, I could only remember how just after the war visiting Czechoslovakia on a British Council tour, I was granted an interview by Benes at the Presidential Palace. In the course of our conversation I asked him whether he wasn't nervous of a Communist coup. He pointed to a telephone on his desk, and said, 'If the Communists are tiresome, I have only to get on the line to my friend Stalin.' Again, at the time of the Hungarian Revolution, friends at the United Nations told me they were sure that the Russians would not dare to do anything so barbarian – in this enlightened international world of ours – as suppress the rising by force.

The invasion did happen and the tanks met no resistance but bare hands.

> How with this rage shall beauty hold a plea,
> Whose action is no stronger than a flower?

But as I write these lines, nearly three months after the invasion, the Czechoslovak universities are being occupied by the students who are quietly staging a sit-down strike. They have also produced a remarkable document, a statement of principles as much as of demands. Among the points they make is that there should be no return to what they call 'Cabinet Policy' (that is to say rule by decree) and that the 'two-way flow of information between the citizens and the leadership' should be maintained. They oppose the censorship and they defend right of assembly and 'freedom of literary and cultural expressions'.

More than ever today, the Czechoslovak students appear as the conscience of freedom in their country. They are this because they have a sense of responsibility without their being burdened with responsibilities. What they do should be an example to all students of the part that they can play: stating demands which at the present moment may seem 'ideal' but which are not removed from reality to the point of being irresponsible and merely provocative. Pledging themselves to stand by these ideal demands. Saying what others say in their hearts but which circumstances may prevent them from saying.

The Berlin Youth Model

To fly from Prague to West Berlin you have to fly to East Berlin and then take a bus through the eastern zone. The imbecility of arrangements of this kind tells one a lot about the politics of east-west relations, those of mutually interacting persecution mania. To go directly from East to West Germany is to experience at first hand the contrast between the absurdity of the east and the absurdity of the west.

The day on which I travelled on an airplane of the DDR, the German Democratic Republic, happened to be one peculiarly rich in the annals of self-parody, Walter Ulbricht's seventy-fifth birthday. The newspapers distributed to us by the blond air hostess were stuffed with articles emulating the exercises in totalitarian oratory parodied by Auden and Isherwood in their socially conscious plays of the Thirties. As a connoisseur of a style which has remained unaltered through the Hitler and Stalin eras to the present day, I particularly enjoyed an article entitled 'At All Times an Ear Open to All' in *Der Morgen*, written by 'Party-Friend Otto Krauss', which opened:

I am often asked, does the President of the State Council, Walter Ulbricht, know exactly how things look from 'down below'? Yes, he does know exactly, more profoundly, than those who ask the question could ever realise. He doesn't rely on information with which he's provided; instead, he seizes on every opportunity to find out what particularly concerns women and men citizens, old as well as young. When he visits a factory he doesn't just talk with the inspectors and engineers, oh no, he slips off into the yard and gets a conversation going with the work folk there, asks each about his particular job, listens to his opinions about The Plan, finds out how much he earns, what he does in his spare time, and keeps an ear open for his grouses and grumbles. He seeks out the comrade peasants in field and stall, and asks them what they think the advantages and disadvantages of the new machinery. . . .

In another article we are informed of the great importance comrade-friend Ulbricht attaches to art and culture. The names of his favourite paintings in a local collection are: Wilhelm Schmied's *Mansfelder Landscape*, Haral Hakenbeck's *Peter in the Park*, Walter Womacka's *On the Beach*, and Paul Michaelin's *The Head Girl*.

The unconscious self-parody corresponding to this in the western Press was the report of a statement made in court by Chancellor Kiesinger that he had not heard of what went on in the Nazi concentration camps till 1945.

The Angst of Berlin is more noticeable today than it was ten years ago. Before the Wall was built, West Berlin seemed to have a rationale: to receive all those refugees escaping into freedom. But today it seems to represent nothing so much as the immense weight of all the money and politics put into it transformed into steel and concrete and automobiles and movies and clothing, all glittering in the harsh artificial light. In its geographical situation, cut off from the west, and not belonging to the east either, Berlin resembles a foreign organ like a heart transplanted into a body which, left with its original heart, would have quickly died. A constant stream of blood transfusions, in the form of money and privileges and visits from cultural organisers, is necessary to keep this pump going. . . .

In contrast to the blatant prosperity overlaying an anxious emptiness which is the tone of the city, the Free University, in the attractive suburb of Dahlem, from which there have risen such trouble and protest, seemed, in late June, astonishingly calm. The students – many of them foreigners – walking along paths under trees, carrying books under their arms, seemed like pre-Columbian (I refer to the historic events connected with the university of that name) students on an American campus. The bureau of the ASTA students' association (*Allgemeiner Studentenausschuss*), in a pleasant villa, with its efficient inhabitants and neatly stacked files, gave a very different impression from the chaos of the Press bureau in the Sorbonne.

The manager of the ASTA office, Seefried Fronius, an attractive young refugee from Rumania, arranged for me to meet some of the representatives of that organisation at the same time as David, the editor of the International Student Conference magazine called *The Student*, was interviewing them.

It was a pleasant meeting in the airy house of rooms full of tables and filing cabinets. It was an atmosphere strangely contrasting with the revolutionary views, and, indeed, the events, discussed.

The conversation bore out a remark Dr Ekkehart Krippendorf had made to me that the German students are stronger on theory than the others. Their views were more clearly formulated and directed toward their aims regarding the university and society than those of the students at Columbia or the Sorbonne. Apart from the mere fact of their being Germans, a reason for this may be that Western Germany is, after all, the result of the fusion of various interests and theories, political and economic, a 'structure' put together, and equally to be analysed and pulled apart, if ever there was one. For various reasons the Free University does seem – much more than the American or French universities – a microcosm of the society: an organisation put together partly from theory (to have a really democratic institution this time!) partly from barely concealed political motive (the western allies' anti-Communism spear-headed in Berlin).

It is hardly surprising then that the students of the SDS (*Sozialistischer Deutscher Studentenbund* – not the American variety) and of ASTA should scarcely differentiate between the university and West Germany beyond it. They regarded the political actions which took up so much of their time at the university as, in fact, their education. One of the students explained: 'We want to break down the traditional concept of the university. To do so, we have to define the social function of the university, and make it into a forum where democracy is discussed and practised. We want to change individual learning into collective learning. We want students and teachers to work together to make a new structure. Students should participate in the administration of the university.' I objected: 'Do you really mean that you want to participate or to control the university?' A boy answered: 'We want no decisions to be taken either against the wishes of the students or against those of the professors. We want participation, not dictatorship, in deciding on lectures, seminars and research projects.'

Foremost in such a programme would be of course the teaching of political science. They wanted to learn political science as experience of the society in which they lived, and having done so, to use this knowledge to change the society.

A girl offered an example which seemed to carry this principle of 'experiencing: learning: transforming' in relation to society rather far when she offered the students' attacks on the Springer publishing establishments as an example of practical education. The others did not take such an extreme view. But all agreed that education (in political science at all events) should be based on experience of actual conditions, theorising about them afterwards, and should be carried on by groups. The group should learn, and the group should examine members of the group – or perhaps not examine them at all (there was disagreement about this) – but decide their qualifications on the basis of what the group knew about them. I suggested that the discipline of examinations taught one to be accurate. A student answered: 'Yes, but learning to be accurate need not necessarily be taught by professors or by an authoritarian personality like about eighty per cent of our professors. It can be achieved by a group discipline. That is what should be changed first, I think. That we abolish this loneliness of all these professors sitting on their chairs.'

David – the editor of *Student* – questioned the rightness of this generation imposing conditions on future generations: 'Supposing the students could choose the professors, well at this point it becomes very important to remember that a student has only a life of four or five years as a student. So therefore you're exposing professors you choose to their being got rid of within four or five years by a reactionary lot of students who might come along. So therefore you have to protect yourselves. You have to protect your own generation as projected within the future and not simply put it at the mercy of every generation of university students who come along.'

The rather predictable answer to this was that new conditions would result in having ideas which were the results of those conditions. It was stated rather dogmatically by a student:

In this situation, it's not a question of generation. The beginning of this movement in all highly industrialised countries and especially the late capitalistic systems of western Europe and the western world is the beginning of mass mobilisation and not the question of one generation within four or five years. If we institute this

86

new model of democracy within the university this will change and turn also the next generation of students. Many students were reactionary and are reactionary – the present and the past. They have not the possibility to practise democracy in their own sphere.

To this, as recorded on the tape of which David kindly sent me a transcript, I replied rather feebly: 'I quite agree with you. I just think at some point, such as electing professors, you have to be careful.'

Today, with tape recorders assisting mirrors, one can catch even the sound of one's voice at unfortunate angles.

Obviously, David asked whether there was a form of society which they deemed their ideal. They said they saw no such 'model' within the western or eastern world of the industrialised countries. They only saw different models in the Third World. Such as Cuba. But they did not think that Cuba provided a model for building a Communist society in a highly industrialised country. They admired Castro and Che because they had made their revolution and in Europe there had been, since the October Revolution, no such revolution. They did not admire the Soviet Union. They thought that although revolutions in Europe and America could not be modelled on Cuba, nevertheless the revolutionised Third World would alter the nature of the 'late-capitalist' countries.

They distrusted the Czechoslovaks because they thought that they admired the west and aimed at establishing in their own country the consumer society of the west. David protested that if this was so, perhaps it was because the Czechs were human beings. It was 'human nature' for people to be acquisitive. The German students replied to this in their usual theoretical vein. People in the socialist countries wanted to be rich not because of human nature but because they were juxtaposed to the richer late-capitalist countries which they wanted to emulate. The argument was that what we call 'human nature' is really man in certain historic contexts which, according to the context, change his demands on life. For example, in the Middle Ages . . . people did not aim at higher living standards. The French Revolution, David protested: 'That was partly a revolution against the fact that the poor were not allowed to expand.' Answer: 'The element of human nature in this context is that anyone who has a developing self-consciousness has the

87

right to participate in the means for developing it which are at his disposal in his world. But that is not human nature. . . .'

We had now got round to planning the revolution and we were able to agree that it was necessary for everybody to have a high living standard. 'It's only possible to liberate yourself if you are already liberated from the common needs of hunger, fear, etc.'

At this point the Czechs might really have been allowed back into the discussion, since what – according to the German student – 'everybody' wants is precisely what they want.

But in describing such a conversation, one has to make allowance for the language difficulty. Most of it was in English and that the German students expressed themselves so well was a tribute to their education. However, even so, what they said about 'human nature' strikes me as irrelevant and unreal. For unless they had said that they were opposed altogether to an industrial society, then they should have accepted the idea of man in an industrial society as that of the 'human nature' to be discussed. Medieval man would have been relevant only if they wished to go back to a medieval society. And within an industrial society man is bound to be acquisitive whether or not he is allowed to acquire things, whether the society is socialist or whether it is what the students of ASTA call 'late-capitalist'. One only has to think of the newest invention to see that this is so. Supposing that a car was invented which not only went along roads but could, cicada-like, sprout helicopter wings, hop over hedges and skim over fields (it will be invented). Nearly everyone would want it, that is all. In the capitalist societies the rich would have it, in the Communist societies, the officials. An industrial society at one end of the scale supports the largest possible population. At the other end of the scale, it provides the rich or privileged with toys. Between the two, the whole contemporary world is trapped. For without in-dustrialism the immense population would die of starvation. The rich and privileged are more easy to dispose of than the poor who are totally dependent on mass production. But as long as you have mass production, you will have both the poor whose existence is made possible by its methods, and you will have acquisitive human nature which will enable some people to have expensive toys.

Paradoxically, when these students discussed what they wanted the university to be, their views were not, in regard to the Free University, entirely revolutionary. They harked back to the ideas which were in the minds of some of those who originated it. And they were remembering legends of what the university had been like in the early Fifties, when there was co-operation between faculty and student.

The Free University was founded in 1948 as West Berlin's answer to the Humboldt University in East Berlin. The word 'free' had two connotations, educational and political. Educationally it meant that the new university would be a forum of discussion between teachers and students, a *Gemeinschaft der Lehrenden und Lernenden*. It was the *Berliner Modell* which would be an example to other institutions of a better relationship between students and faculty than had existed in the old German universities. These had not been reformed, they had been 'restored' after the war. The Berlin model was to do away with the feudal university of lordly professors, attentive assistants, and underling students wondering whether after three years at the university they might have an interview with the professor who would decide their whole future.

The political connotation of the word 'free' was meant to contrast western freedom with the lack of freedom of the students in East Berlin. This worked well so long as there was Stalin and after him the walled-in East to be dramatically free of. During the Stalinist period freedom meant anti-Communism, helping refugees from the East. In the early days of the Wall it meant digging tunnels, helping people to escape. However, more recently, the students began to become aware of freedoms to defend both abroad and nearer home. There is a rather formidable list of things which *Der Konvent* (the student parliament) and its executive committee (ASTA) found they cared about. There was Vietnam, German rearmament, the relations of West Germany with the eastern zone, the joining by the German Socialist Party (the SPD, to which the SDS had once been close) of the Grand Coalition of the West German government. Beyond all this was the vast array of forces which produced the Economic Miracle, the most blatant show put on by the Consumer Society.

Meanwhile the Berlin model of the teaching and learning

community (which I observed when it was still being practised in halls and cinemas, before the university was installed on its present campus) disappeared under the enormous anonymous overcrowding of the university. As a consequence of this expansion the founders had to abandon their original aim of only selecting professors who shared the ideals of democratic interchange, and take professors from older universities who were far from sympathetic to an academic community with a student parliament, members of whose executive committee were dedicated to defending the right of students to interpret the word *'frei'* as meaning that *Der Konvent* could make pronouncements about state and international politics, just as if it were a real parliament. This exercise became extremely unpopular when in 1962 the students started collecting money for Algerian students who were resisting the French. The students had started interpreting political freedom in ways that embarrassed the western occupying powers. The students, on their side, remembered how no one had protested when they raised funds for refugee students from the eastern zone. Assistance for the Algerians was forbidden by the rector of the university.

After this there was a series of incidents of the kind that rebelling students everywhere collect, file, annotate, publish and distribute to other students, like Coriolanus displaying his wounds. Thus in 1965 the rector banned the well-known journalist Erich Kuby from speaking on the campus on the occasion of the twentieth anniversary of the defeat of Nazi Germany. Seven years previously Kuby had said that the university had been given the name 'free' only as a point in the polemics against the 'unfreedom' of the Humboldt University. The ban resulted in widespread protests by students. There followed the many protests against the war in Vietnam. These were followed in turn by the academic senate forbidding political demonstrations in the university. At that the ASTA committee resigned. Next, the ban was withdrawn. There were further political protests, etc., etc., etc.

I have already described how this led to the tragic shooting of one of the protesting students, Benno Ohnesorg.

On 8 June, more than half the students of the university marched through the streets accompanying Ohnesorg's funeral

90

procession to the city boundaries. He was buried in Hanover where with the permission of the East German authorities the students held a congress on the 'Organisation of Opposition' in his memory. The remarkable document recording the discussion is published under the title *Bedingungen und Organisation des Widerstandes* (Voltaire Flugschrift).

Nearly a year later, Easter 1968, there followed the attempted assassination of Rudi Dutschke, one of the most thoughtfully analytic of the student revolutionaries, but not the least provocative, who was shot by a young painter belonging to no political party. This was one of those acts of violence that spring out of an atmosphere by now electric with fear and hatred. The students attributed this evil climate to their powerful opponents of the Springer Press, whose newspapers have a near monopoly of the Press in Berlin, and a great empire of publications throughout the rest of West Germany. Reacting violently, they started a whole series of attacks on office buildings of the Springer organisation in many towns of Germany. Buildings were occupied, stones were thrown, cars were thrown over on their sides and burned. The police responded with violence that probably exceeded that of the students.

Since these events, the students have become much preoccupied with the question of violence. In May, when there was an international meeting of students at the London School of Economics, Dr Krippendorf, one of the German representatives, declared that the question of violence (like the question 'How much is permitted to be consumed in the non-consumer society?') was one which the students should not be drawn into answering, since the violence justified would depend on the violence met with, so that no rules could be laid down about what means might or might not be permitted. However, the anxiety shown by many of the students about violence shows that many of them would regard this answer as evasive. Neal Ascherson, formerly Berlin correspondent of *The Observer*, described to me an interview with students in which, pressed by journalists, they attempted to formulate conditions in which it would be justified to throw stones, or apples, depending on the hardness of the apple. He said that the death of two of their number had come as a much greater shock to the German students than to the French, who took the consequences of

91

violence in their stride. However, if one reads the SDS publications one sees that they have frequently recommended provocations of the police as a strategy for 'unmasking' the violence of the authorities.

The trouble with violence is that it leads to doubletalk in which the provocateur is playing at one and the same time the role of assailant and victim. It is hardly surprising that the German students are now, with much concern, debating among themselves the question of violence.

With the German students of the SDS, one begins to understand the meaning of the word 'alienation'. In a city many of whose inhabitants are paid not to leave it, students are brought in from the outside. To them, once they have set themselves in opposition, the German establishment must seem a gigantic conspiracy to let sleeping dogs lie while those who have benefited from the economic miracle, and the American support of West Germany, hang on to their gains. To the general public (including the workers), which does not want to be disturbed, the students must seem yapping puppies. The two sides of the Berlin Wall, the Communist and the western, are equally impervious to the students' appeals.

Some of the leaders, like Dutschke and Krippendorf, have come from the eastern zone. Such men are in the position of being twice disillusioned, by the east and by the west, by the Communists and by the anti-Communists. Inevitably they pursue some third ideology, from Mao's China or Castro's Cuba. They pursue it with the energy of Pirandello's six characters in search of an author.

Essays by Rudi Dutschke and Wolfgang Lefevre in the volume *Rebellion der Studenten* (Rowohlt) follow a pattern which might be termed that of the politics of extreme isolation. First, a search to rearrange the order of ancestors; second, to realign the forces of the contemporary world. In the first part, the problem is to bypass Stalin and nearly all the governments of eastern Europe, and get back to the pure doctrine of Marx and Lenin (by way of Marcuse), the untainted practice of Communist martyrs like Liebknecht and Rosa Luxemburg. In the second part, the forces opposing one another in the modern world have to be rearranged in a purer ideological and moral order. Marx's thesis of class struggle has to be converted into

92

a vision of struggle between the forces of neo-capitalism – the consumer society – and an alliance of Maoists, Castroites, the impoverished Third World of the underdeveloped countries, and students. In this interpretation of the past and present situation, the consumer society of 'neo-capitalism' is characterised by the phrase 'manipulation': it is no longer, like early capitalism, simply oppressive. By satisfying the needs of the workers up to the point where they feel themselves one of the forces competing in the society, it lulls them into thinking that they are enjoying real freedom. The task of the students is 'to awake the con-sciousness' of the workers to their situation. It is for them to persuade the workers that they are not really free, and to make them see that neo-capitalism is still a society of war, hunger, and exploitation of the Third World.

These positions are ideological in the most revolutionary – or neo-revolutionary – sense of the word. They are theoretical to that point where theory seems sometimes to merge into a persecution complex (but then all revolutionary theories have an element of persecution complex about them). What is both moving and disquieting is the sense they give one of the isolation of intelligent and vital minds (forget for the moment that they are called students) in Germany, the centre of Europe.

The note of persecution occasionally broke through the calm conversation with the ASTA students on the campus of the Free University that beautiful afternoon. Everything in the office, with the neatly arranged papers, the bright light outside, the students who despite their casual dress – perhaps because of it – seemed elegant and stylish compared with people garishly dressed in Berlin, seemed reassuring. Then suddenly, amid the theorising and the rather remote descriptions of events, a girl broke out in a strained voice, and explained how after the attempt to murder the student leader Rudi Dutschke in the spring, there followed attacks by the students on the establish-ments of the Springer Press which – the students thought – had so maligned them. 'We tried to make clear the situation of Berlin which the politicians give such an hysterical picture of. The politicians don't explain the economic situation, they try to make the people enemies of the students. The first enemy was the Communist people – now the enemy is made to be the student. The people were beginning to reflect seriously about

93

THE YEAR OF THE YOUNG REBELS

their problems. Now they say the students are the motive for the bad political situation and economic situation; that, on account of the students, industry doesn't want to invest any more here. So we had to explain to the Berlin people our own democratic demands, and to explain the special situation in Berlin. We formed many political groups. The students, young workers and pupils who are living in the same district made one political group and distributed leaflets. It's the first time we have ever worked together with the young workers. This all happened between Easter and May. On May 1st we demonstrated and the demonstration included about thirty thousand people – the biggest to be held in Berlin.'

The spring of 1968 seems to have been the high point of there being any wide support for the German students. Already when I was in Berlin there was an encroaching sense of isolation. The students at ASTA were talking about the past. When I walked up the enormous length of the Kurfürstendamm to call at the offices of the SDS I found them deserted. A few days later I went to Frankfurt and visited the offices of the SDS there. I found the student leader Kurt Dietrich Wolff sitting in an empty office. He remarked sadly that there was no communication between the German workers and students corresponding to the relationship of the students with the young workers in France.

It is often said that the young Germans of today are a post-Hitler, post-war, post-post-war generation, and in them all those traumas have been wiped out. They are the first generation of Germans since 1933 to have been born into a free and prosperous Germany. This may be so, but I think their isolation relates to these things just the same. For to an older generation – after a short period when the liberals tried to understand their grievances – they provided a recurrent nightmare – the spectre of the young Communists – even the young Nazis – rising up in the Thirties. Their movement is partly in reaction against the densely thick surface prosperity of the West Germans of the 'Economic Miracle' behind which the past is hidden as behind a wall. Prosperous Germany, so different from France, nevertheless has its own deafening silences, and the students, who are of the Adenauer generation have a desire to break the heavy dumbness and deafness with talk, just as do the French generation of the young under de Gaulle.

During our conversation with the students at the *Freie Universität*, one of them remarked, rather strangely, that in Germany the leftists had never been violent and had never responded to violence against them, because they were too weak to face up to a fight. He added that the student uprisings were the first occasion in the history of the German Federal Republic that students and young workers had resorted to physical violence.

So when the West German students talk about 'consciousness' they also mean, I think, 'conscience'. Despite their being such a new generation, they still represent a lingering German bad conscience about the recent past. They react against the overwhelming impression produced by West Germany of bad conscience richly bought off. The students are isolated and they are resented, not just on account of their violence, but because they are reminders. As well as having the look of the unprecedented new young, they also have the look of ghosts risen from hastily covered graves.

Politics of the Non-Political

The Moral Immoralists

In ordinary times, most people think of politics as proceeding through the established political channels of the society. If they live in a society where there is only one party then these may be cells or local branches in factory or village where they are permitted – within the limits of their not challenging the party's general policy – to state their views. In a multi-party system they choose between different general lines of policy held by the different parties.

In ordinary times, student political life provides a miniature of the political life of the whole society. Thus in the countries of eastern Europe (the People's Democracies) the students belong to youth organisations which have branches, cells, etc. for political discussion of, or instruction in, the party's policy, Communist theory, and so on.

In the universities in the democracies, there is voluntary organisation, usually among the students themselves, of political life, along the lines of the policies of the different parties. For instance, at English universities there are student Labour, Liberal and Conservative clubs.

In what I call here an ordinary (i.e. unrevolutionary) situation the students will tend to think of their political associations as paths leading to the political life of the world beyond the university.

If they distinguish themselves in these organisations they may the more easily become career politicians later on. In Communist countries the youth leaders of the Komsomol, or of the youth organisations in the People's Republics, may draw attention to their potentialities as political leaders. In England the Conservative, Labour and Liberal parties are thick with the dead wood of men who were once office holders in the Oxford University Union – that training ground for the rhetoric of feigned sincerity and feigned indignation in which

99

Mr Edward Heath, the present Conservative Party Leader, so excels.

In ordinary circumstances politics is regarded as the activity of professionals, and only the occasional concern of voters, who are quite content to discover their own views in the declared programmes of the political parties. This does not mean that sometimes politics, moving along its lines like public highways, cannot be impassioned. There can be deep differences between the parties in a democracy, and deep passions behind the one party in a Communist country. In the nineteenth century Gladstone and Disraeli, the two leaders of the opposed English Liberal and Conservative parties, could even have the satisfaction of regarding one another as wickedly immoral. When I was a child the feud between the Conservative protectionists and the Liberal free traders was carried on with a religious fervour only equalled by that between Catholics and Protestants.

An extraordinary situation I call one in which a number of people, sufficient to make their protest felt, no longer think the established or conventional political channels right for voicing their demands. In such situations they are likely to condemn the whole system and to count their condemnation as moral. They call the system, which they reject, immoral; indeed it seems a conspiracy invented for the purpose of not admitting their moral demands.

That the morals of the rebels, and of their cause, may be regarded as highly debatable by those who do not support them, is irrelevant to my argument. Indeed the rebels may defiantly proclaim and show themselves as immoral as possible in terms of the conventional 'establishment' which they regard as hypocritical. The important thing is that the rebels see a conflict between their moral cause and the immoral one of the official leaders. Even if, like some doctrinaire Marxists, they consider themselves indifferent to morals in a struggle which is between historic forces, in fact in their rhetoric they will fall constantly into depicting their struggle as that between good and evil. If, like the Beatniks, the Hippies and Yippies, the rebels appear to themselves, as to others to be immoralists in their private behaviour, by virtue of their opposition to the bad cause, they will appear to themselves moral in their public behaviour. Private vices will be washed clean as snow by their public virtue.

'Anti-bourgeois' is the battle cry of the rebels. For the bourgeois is the exact opposite of someone whose private 'immorality' is cancelled out by his public 'morality'. The bourgeois thinks that his private virtue justifies his public attitudes which he judges by different standards.

The situation of the good society 'struggling to be born' against the bad society is comprehensible to most people if it is enclosed within a 'revolutionary situation'; that is to say if there is the revolt of an oppressed class against the oppressors, breaking out at a time when there is a major national crisis, resulting perhaps from defeat in war and the collapse of the economy.

What seemed remarkable – and to some observers rather shocking – about the students' revolt was that it happened against no such background of a revolutionary situation. This contributed to the sense of unreality which many witnesses experienced in the spring of 1968, at the time of the Columbia and the Sorbonne uprisings and the riots in Berlin. It was difficult for them to believe altogether in either the revolution or the revolutionaries. The April and May revolution somehow seemed 'dreamed up'.

And yet what the revolt did show was that people may protest against the society in which they live and even strive for revolution on grounds which are not generally accepted as reasons for revolution.

Western and Eastern Freedom

There is one case in which most people would find a revolutionary cause justified even without there being a revolutionary situation. That is when rebels demand freedom. Throughout history people have revolted in the name of freedom – whether they mean by this freedom of self-expression or national independence. The revolt of the Czech students was quite comprehensible. They were supporting a traditional struggle for freedom, a twentieth-century version of those great struggles for self-expression and independence of oppressed peoples which took place in the nineteenth century.

As a matter of fact there was a sense in which, as I shall

try to explain, the western students felt the lack of freedom. That they should have done so is a matter of irony for the Czechs and for intellectuals in eastern Europe, but freedom is after all comparative. There comes a stage when freedom is not just freedom to express yourself but to be able to change conditions. If you have freedom but at the same time it is clear to you that the exercise of it will never change conditions which you regard as evil then you may feel your only real freedom must lie in rebellion.

The atmosphere of Gaullist France is repressive. Government control of the mass media, particularly of television, was one of the grievances taken up by the students in May. In Gaullist France – despite the general's talk about 'participation' – there is a sense of distance between the government and the governed which suggests that the political leadership continues on its iron course completely unhearing the voices of the thinkers and men of imagination. The great age of the general, on his icy pinnacle, dramatised for the young, who passionately care about justice and freedom, the sense of the utter remoteness of the government.

In a country where there is almost complete freedom from censorship and where there are no open forms of repression people may nevertheless feel powerless to oppose public evil. The sense of impotence is exacerbated by the difficulty of explaining why it is felt.

Recently Miss Mary McCarthy, discussing the case of Galanskov and Ginsburg, pointed out, rather wistfully, that somehow protest in Russia and the People's Democracies seems more effective than protest in the west. What she meant is that in the Communist countries protest produces some kind of result even if it is a repressive one: for the spoken and the written word are more respected. But in the western democracies it simply echoes forlornly and unheeded down the vistaed corridors of power.

So in the west the feeling is that although there is freedom it is ineffective. It is surrounded by a vacuum. Society is arranged in concentric circles so that the inhabitants of each circle talk only to one another, like voices in a whispering gallery, but never reach the inner circles of power. The intellectuals speak to other intellectuals, the poets read the poems of

102

POLITICS OF THE NON-POLITICAL

other poets. No phrase has more mocked at the imagination
than Shelley's about the poets being the unacknowledged
legislators of mankind.

American writers are perhaps at heart Shelleyans and have
never quite accepted the idea that the imagination has nothing
to say about public affairs. They may not, like Walt Whitman,
want to guide the democracy, but all the same they wish to feel
that poetic consciousness in some sense represents the whole
democracy, and, even if hiddenly and secretly, influences it.
With part of his mind the American writer has been driven to
regard himself as a member of an élite, and as such he has
acquired a certain arrogance. Yet he never forgets that the
penalty of being a member of a literary élite is exclusiveness
which means being excluded as well as excluding. He would
like, on some existential plane of his expressed consciousness,
to be equal to the whole breathing conscious acting democracy.
A furious gale blows through American literature which is that
of the universal American poetic voice demanding to be heard.
Recently it has got much angrier, its language more violent
and obscene.

The obscenity of Henry Miller is that of the frustrated
prophet. It is probably the most influential current in underground American literature, and has flowed into the estuary of
language, extraordinarily uninhibited, unrestrained and in-
decent, which has swept on to the stages of theatres off
Broadway and which flows out of the mouths of hundreds of
bearded, blue-jeaned or leather-jerkined, pot-smoking students,
male and female. Like the French movement of the *enragés* the
American student movement is literary even when it may
appear illiterate, as is apparent in the conclusion of the open
letter of Mark Rudd, the SDS Columbia student leader, to the
president of the university, Grayson Kirk: 'There is only one
thing left to say. It may sound nihilistic to you, since it is the
opening shot in a war of liberation. I'll use the words of Leroi
Jones, whom I'm sure you don't like a whole lot: "Up Against the
Wall, motherfucker, this is a stick-up". Yours for freedom,
Mark.'

If this seems extraordinary language for a student to use
when addressing his university president, it should be remembered that it is a literary quotation.

103

Far more obviously, the French movement with its exhortations to imagination to take power, and with its surrealist slogans, was an assertion through the speeches and actions of the young, of a literary consciousness desiring to have some say in politics in a situation which was *felt*, rather than rationally *thought*, to be oppressive. And in spite of lack of censorship and the right of the French to say whatever they choose, Gaullism was repressive, as Michel Crozier, Professor of Sociology at the University of Paris at Nanterre, points out:[1]

This rigid – apparently modern but in reality conservative – Gaullist bureaucratic state had suppressed all these indirect channels for settling grievances and introducing innovations. It boasted of courage and clarity, but could ignore and neglect problems that would have brought down any government of the Fourth Republic. Which means that it was to be completely helpless when, finally, a major crisis became the only solution to these problems.

The spring fever of talk which overtook not only the students but almost everyone in Paris seemed so like the euphoria of camaraderie and open-heartedness which overtakes people after revolution, that many people mistook it for this. The fact that it was permitted made it very difficult to explain why it had this look of freedom gained.

In fact part of the talk was the attempt of the students to explain to themselves the situation in which they were free to talk about freedom while they did not feel free. They were free it seemed only to define their sense of the lack of freedom. There are moments when this led them to think – as it did Miss Mary McCarthy from whom I have quoted – that to have apparent but ineffective freedom might be a worse state than to have none at all.

Students look to writers like Marcuse to analyse and explain – to 'justify' – their sense of frustration which they feel in a world in which they are a privileged minority, and where they enjoy a great deal of freedom. They want it explained to them that the whole democracy, with its governing class, big business, mass media, is a vast conspiracy of powers that makes their freedoms illusory.

These writers seem at first an odd mixture; on the one

[1] *The Public Interest*, Fall 1968 (no. 13).

hand, the Henry Miller who gives an account of America as *The Air-conditioned Nightmare* in his book of that name, or in his wonderful essay on American bread, which expands into a condemnation of a whole civilisation; on the other hand, a political scientist like Marcuse who analyses the consumer society as a system in which everyone is conditioned by the cycle of over-production of consumer goods kept going by the creation of artificial needs in the minds of consumers. The French student leaders deny that they have studied Marcuse; but they have certainly been influenced by the explanation that modern society conditions people's thinking and feeling so that they involuntarily respond to its requirements. They would agree with the following passage from the essay on 'Aggressiveness in Advanced Industrial Society' (in the volume entitled *Negations*):

As for the systematic manipulation and control of the psyche in the advanced industrial society, manipulation and control for what, and by whom? Over and above all particular manipulation in the interest of certain businesses, policies, lobbies – the general objective purpose is to reconcile the individual with the mode of existence which his society imposes on him.

Sociology and Hell

It is significant that many of the militant students have studied sociology, because it is above all the sociologists who describe the effects of social conditioning on the individual. The individual whose values, tastes and thoughts are the projections of the environment in which he lives is – as poets from Baudelaire to T. S. Eliot have pointed out – in Hell; for the people in the *Inferno* are there because they have become totally conditioned by their material desires. They have been 'sold' damnation by the world, the flesh and the devil, just as much as people today are sold their needs – and ultimately what they are in their inmost being – by advertising.

Any analysis of individuals as having aims and values which are the result of their social conditioning is bound, I think, to produce a revulsion from people who have a strong sense of their own life. Such people refuse to recognise themselves as

105

conditioned in the jobs they choose, whom they marry, the things they buy or do not buy, their values, and even in what they think and are, by social and economic circumstances. Consumer reports, definitions of character based on the classification of physiological types, and indeed any type-casting of individuals according to statistics, will repel them by suggesting that the individual is a 'social unit', a conditioned automaton. Thus sociology is the toxin which produces an anti-toxin: insistence on the concept of individual consciousness which is unconditioned or which can cut through the conditions.

D. H. Lawrence put this very forcefully when he wrote an essay on John Galsworthy. Lawrence saw Galsworthy as a novelist who was attempting to write the sociology of the Forsytes, the typical upper-middle class English rich. Lawrence's criticism is that Galsworthy, having created the Forsytes as sociological types, falls in love with them, instead of satirising them for their failure to be anything but types – to be human beings: 'When one reads Mr Galsworthy's books it seems as if there were not on earth one single human individual. They are all these social beings, positive and negative. There is not a free soul among them.'

Lawrence's reaction is that of a poet: for poetry is concerned with unconditioned individual life and not with life as the product of social conditioning. If Dante had been a sociologist and not a poet, he would have been content to describe the inhabitants of the *Inferno* as types projected by those conditions which had resulted from their listening to Satan's sales' talk. But since he was a poet he was concerned with how unconditioned consciousness had got into Hell and how it could be liberated into the life of the imagination.

Sociologists – or rather those writers who work in a kind of twilight world between sociology, politics and psychology – play a peculiar role in our world. They are the theologians of our secular society, quite innocently, and with a feeling that we should rejoice in them, writing their accounts of the materialist hells in which we have chosen to live – the worlds of *The Hidden Persuaders*, *The Status Seekers*, *The Managerial Society*, *The Affluent Society*, *The Organization Man*, *The Warfare State*, etc.

But whoever is what Lawrence calls a 'free soul' will only have to read the sociologists' account of his automatic reactions

106

to his automatic conditioning, to wish to prove that he is a free human being. The others may be conditioned – the bourgeois – but he is a 'free soul'. Hence once the society has been described as one in which:

the productive apparatus tends to become totalitarian to the extent to which it determines not only the socially needed occupations, skills, and attitudes, but also individual needs and aspirations (Marcuse)

then the word revolution means not an alternative system, another ideology, but a key which will unlock the present systematisation, and release those who are alive within the prison into consciousness, imagination, love.

And for this reason also the students are almost childishly (preserving after all what is childlike in them from the conditioned adult world) unwilling to define the conditions, the ideas, the programme of the revolution. As Cohn-Bendit told Jean-Paul Sartre:[1]

Our movement's strength is precisely that it is based on an 'uncontrollable' spontaneity, that it gives an impetus without trying to canalise it or use the action it has unleashed to its own profit. There are clearly two solutions open to us today. The first would be to bring together half a dozen people with political experience, ask them to formulate some convincing immediate demands, and say, 'Here is the student movement, do what you like with it'. This is the bad solution. The second is to try to give an understanding of the situation not to the totality of demonstrators but to a large number of them. To do so we must avoid building an organisation immediately, or defining a programme; that would inevitably paralyse us.

In this insistence on the student movement as revolutionary improvisation directed towards a goal of perpetual change called The Revolution, there is something self-protective, a fear of falling into the traps of previous revolutions, of isolated aesthetic individualism, of the Russian Revolution, of the Thirties. The students do not trust Russian and eastern Europeans any more than Americans and western Europeans, and they do not want to repeat the mistakes of the Thirties. But

[1] The Cohn-Bendit quotation is from his interview with Jean-Paul Sartre, quoted in Hervé Bourges (ed), *The Student Revolt*, London (Cape) 1968 (also Panther Books).

they do not want to be completely free individuals either. They are too politically involved, too politically conscious, to become lone wolf individualists like D. H. Lawrence. They would probably regard the highly individualistic position of a D. H. Lawrence, an E. E. Cummings, or a Henry Miller fighting all organised groups, as another trap. They are too conscious of the leaders of the Thirties, who now sit in offices in Warsaw and Budapest or who are the older generation of writers in Paris, to accept Moscow Communism or variants of it in Belgrade, Prague or Bucharest. They want to be free in the sense that their commitment to their cause always remains 'voluntary', but they want also to have connections with some wider movement of the workers, with some free-developing spontaneous Marxist revolution or guerilla movement of Mao or Castro or Che Guevara. So they try to win over the young workers to their position, which is no position, and they yearn for their broadest and furthest base to be the 'Third World'.

The Third World as Revolutionary Situation

Thus a German student at the *Freie Universität* of Berlin told me: 'The successful revolution in the Third World will have some influence on the development of the highly industrialised countries. The emancipation of South America, for example, will have a very great influence on the development of North America. The emancipation of the Third World will also change the resources of the highly industrialised societies.'

The Third World is called in then to provide the revolutionaries of the west with the revolutionary situation which is lacking in their own countries. As Cohn-Bendit remarked in the interview with Jean-Paul Sartre, from which I have quoted, the conditions for revolution, which are those of serious economic crisis, converging with an active movement of workers as well as students, do not exist today, and, as a consequence 'we have to struggle forward on the basis of a global challenge'.

The students in the west do well to concern themselves with the Third World. Indeed, they can be criticised for not doing so seriously, when they simply invoke the concept of vast areas where there is a real revolutionary situation and class struggle in order to provide their own struggle in quite different circumstances with the context of a global 'revolutionary situation'. If they were really concerned with the Third World they would talk more about problems which concern it and less about tactics of guerilla revolutionary war which they may borrow from it. They would discuss nutrition, illiteracy and population, in which they seem to take very little interest.

Yet if one looks from the abstraction of the 'global challenge' back at the universities themselves, one sees that in fact the grievances of the western students have very little in common with those of students in Latin America, Japan, India or the middle east. I have visited Indian universities – one has only to go to them to see that they are young peoples' slums: thousands on thousands of impoverished students with the same non-standard of life as the people in the streets and fields, where they eat and sleep and fall dead.

The students of the west cannot convincingly identify their situation with that of students in the Third World and make it their revolutionary situation. For the fact is that 'situation' here means 'circumstances' and their circumstances are vastly different. The world really does not, in a social or a political sense, provide a situation which is global. There are a lot of separate situations in which people, some of them students, in different parts of the world are trapped. The students should understand what this means. They do not have to behave as though they, living in New York, Paris or Berlin, were Indians in Bombay or Calcutta. They have to try to understand what it would mean to be in the situation of Indians and how different it is from theirs. As things are, they seem incapable of understanding even what it means to be a student in Prague or Brno (there is no reference in Cohn-Bendit's book[1] to Czechoslovakia); and they talk as though it is remiss of the Czech students not to have the same aims and ideas as French, American and West German students.

So the western students are enclosed by their situation which is that of living in societies where there are too many commodities rather than too few and where the state is organised in the interest of producing things. If there were a

[1] Daniel Cohn-Bendit, *Obsolete Communism: the left-wing alternative*, London (André Deutsch) 1968.

revolution in the west it would inevitably have to be different from the revolutions that may happen in the Third World. It would be a revolution not for the means but for the values of living, not for basic freedom but for the exercise of freedom against the direct interests of the society. It would be a revolution not of the interested but of the disinterested.

The Word 'Revolution'

Critics of the students think that they are not 'justified' in being revolutionaries because (1) they are not an oppressed class; (2) they have rhetoric and they make demonstrations, but they use no conventional revolutionary strategy. In fact they themselves disclaim any ambitions to set up a dictatorship with leaders; (3) there has been no revolutionary situation since 1945 and perhaps it is wishful thinking to suppose that there will be one; (4) of their emphasis on the revolution as a way of life, rather than on the 'Day of the Revolution' when they seize power.

The students both try and do not try to justify their revolution in terms of a revolutionary stereotype. Daniel Cohn-Bendit's famous interview with Jean-Paul Sartre made during the events of May is revealing of this ambivalence.[1]

It is Sartre, the dissector of all politics, writer of the Thirties, the old ideologue anatomising ideological situations, who starts off by describing the situation as a 'revolutionary one'. Cohn-Bendit takes a much cooler view. He thinks that the results of the uprising are greater than could have been anticipated. Even now though the most that the movement could expect to do would be to overthrow the Gaullist regime. He realises however that the students cannot achieve this by themselves as to do so they would need the support of the Communist Party and the trades union organisations. He does not think that the May uprising will lead to a revolution or anything like it: at best to a return to power of the French left, from which he does not expect much; probably what he calls a 'Wilson-style' government.

He does not represent the students as an oppressed class.

[1] Hervé Bourges (ed), *The Student Revolt*, London (Cape) 1968 (also Panther Books).

110

He thinks of them as 'leaven' rather than as a vanguard. They have to abandon the theory of the 'leading vanguard' and replace it by that of 'the active minority functioning as a permanent leaven, pushing for action without ever leading it'. He says 'we are moving towards a perpetually changing society, modified by revolutionary actions at each stage'.

This is a reference of course to the Third World, where there are oppressors and oppressed. Moreover, as the students of the German SDS pointed out, if you look at things globally the capitalist world can be regarded as oppressing the Third World in a global class struggle.

The students are an international movement (today, 'the international' perhaps) and communicate awareness of this. Cohn-Bendit remarks that some people think that the Third World will bring about the collapse of the capitalist world; others that 'only thanks to revolution in the capitalist world can the Third World advance'.

The students are only the active minority who light the fuse. This, indeed, they did in Paris in May and June. But having lit it, they became absorbed into the wider movement. Cohn-Bendit adds that the Bolshevik Party did not ' "lead" the Russian Revolution' but was 'borne along by it'.

One has at the end the general impression that Cohn-Bendit believes much more in revolutionaries than he cares about the revolution. He describes the aim of the revolutionaries as being not a reformed capitalist society, 'but launching an experiment that completely breaks with that society, an experiment that will not last, but which allows a glimpse of a possibility; something which is revealed for a moment and then vanishes. But that is enough to prove that that something could exist'. This poetic statement sounds closer to utopianism than to Marxist-Leninism.

The movement has a spontaneity which is uncontrollable. And it does not try to use the action it has 'unleashed to its own profit'. This distinguishes the student movement very sharply from that of the workers who, according to the theory of the class war, certainly are not disinterested. The disinterestedness of the students is in the interest of the workers.

I have already remarked that the students' movement is hedged round with inhibitions. When it comes to considering

111

the nature of the revolution, they are afraid of its having those features of bureaucratisation, paternalism (or worse), authoritarianism, which characterise the system they are fighting, and which in fact – except when they look to their dreams of the Red Guards or Castroism – characterise Communist as much as capitalist society. What they want above all is perpetual change, perpetual spontaneity.

Despite their attachment to the idea of the class struggle they are ambiguous about the workers. On the one hand, revolution is unthinkable without them. On the other hand, the old workers are set in their ways, too rigid, as trade unionists and as Communist Party members. There is mutual distrust between the students and them. So it is to the young workers that they turn and whom they hope to convert. These are more young than they are workers. They are asked by the students to forget that they are workers and to come into the planned communal university. Side by side with talk of revolution, there is talk of restaurants and cafeterias:

On university restaurants we have a demand which is basic. We demand their abolition as university restaurants. They must become youth restaurants in which all young people, whether students or not, can eat for one franc forty.

What Cohn-Bendit means is that the young workers should be invited to come into the universities, not just to eat but also to sleep: 'Let us welcome them to the *Cités* where the rent is from nine thousand to ten thousand francs per month. And let the well-to-do students in law and *sciences-po* go elsewhere.'

This does not sound very feasible – there would be a lot of crowding – but it is the attitude that matters. Evidently if the young workers came to eat and sleep at the university they would be scarcely distinguishable from students, particularly from the political scientists and sociologists. And the workers would be talking to them about the same things as the students were learning at the university. Students and young workers would be united in the movement of spontaneity.

If one envisages a classical revolution planned by a ruthless minority with a very definite programme and remorselessly directed against a class enemy, all this sounds, in the long run, evasive. The appeal to the Third World to play the role of proletariat in a global class conflict is unconvincing because the deprived populations of Asia, Africa and South America are too divided by race, colour, religion and mutual prejudices against one another to achieve a unity in any foreseeable future. The appeal to the workers to form a dough in which the students will be the leaven leaves one wondering whether in the long run the bourgeois students will be better received by the workers than the white students at Columbia were by the blacks. For those to whom they go over do not particularly want them. Workers and blacks have to be persuaded to accept them, and then not as leaders, in a movement which the students may have to persuade the workers to lead. White students at Columbia University joined the black students when, together, they took Hamilton Hall, and then were asked to leave. The relations of the white students at Berkeley with the extremist Black Panthers was uneasy. The Sorbonne students tried to join the workers but the workers received them coolly and sometimes even barred them out, though they did win over some of the young workers. The students of the German SDS, who with their insistence on theory regard the workers as the true army of the revolution, do not have good relations with them.

The students obviously feel uneasy about all these things. As we see, they try to construct for themselves a situation in which the students represent the conscious avant garde of the revolution. By making out that their movement is part of a global revolution in which the struggle of oppressed and oppressors is still continuing, they cling to the view that capitalist society will break down and produce a revolutionary situation.

In this way, although opposed to the bureaucratic Communist parties they try to put themselves back into the Marxist picture of a Communist revolution.

Yet there are differences, not only in their situation, but also in their attitudes, which alter the whole significance of their movement.

They are not primarily concerned with seizing power, and it is difficult to see how they could be, unless they were to merge

113

their identity as students into some longer term revolutionary movement. They do not consider the aim of their revolution to be victory over the current establishment, followed by the setting up of a dictatorship.

There is a sense of forces moving through their rhetoric which is more convincing than their attempts to fit spontaneity into patterns of revolutionary situation. Their revolutionary idea is, as I have written above, moral passion. The essential is that they regard the society against which they are rebelling as intolerable to their sense of life, for which 'spontaneity', 'participation', etc., are the names. Since they believe this to be so then they will also believe that there is a level of being, or of experience, on which everyone who has eyes to see, will agree with them. The living can respond but the dead can not. But the living who are the young are a pervasive consciousness. The young workers have to be persuaded that they and the students share one life.

'The Production' and Generations

There is much discussion about the 'generation gap', that division between young and old all human generations must endure. There is an idea current that it has widened recently. An explanation often put forward for this is that the young are remote from the environment which conditions their parents, just as they themselves are conditioned by the new environment.

Within limits, there is perhaps some truth in this. The whole environment does not condition or change people as much as might be expected, but fragments of it do. Bits of the changed environment do change people, whereas other bits, which may in themselves be startlingly new, do not. I doubt whether rockets exploring space have changed anyone except the scientists most directly concerned. There are reasons for thinking that the exploration of the moon will have much less effect on the human imagination than did the exploration, in Elizabethan times, of the New World.

But television has changed people, and if there is any physiological or psychological reality in the 'generation gap' it may be that a generation brought up on television is different

114

from preceding ones. By this I do not mean that the young have been changed by having all those shootings and other horrors going on in the box in their front parlours. I mean that television has changed people's attitude to publicity. The public image walks and talks in the living room as does also the private image made public in this intimate and private box. So the television has contributed to the general modern journalistic tendency of making the private life public property; but paradoxically, by making it at the same time the private property of millions of people. The effect of this has been to diminish the space between private and public worlds. People can be seen on television behaving in an entirely personal way, retaining all their private characteristics and yet being treated to unprecedented publicity.

The Beatniks were perhaps the first generation who, reacting against the public attitudes of the 'square' people of their time, nevertheless – all the bearded privacy of their strange attire, their dope, their pads, their girls, their incoherence – became television stars. And they did so without self-consciousness or loss of integrity. It is as though Thoreau, having renounced civilisation and gone to live in his hut at Walden, had projected the austere image of his self-punishing, delighted solitude into a million viewers' homes. And the remarkable thing is that if this hero of theirs had been of the Beatnik generation he might well have combined a passion for solitude with a love of being televised. Writing his journal was, after all, the first step along the way to instantaneous self-imagisation.

The militant students may then be different from previous rebels in that they not only demonstrate but their demonstrations while being authentic are also a performance. This was brought home to me in March when I happened to be in Washington at the time of the famous riots in the Negro ghetto. I heard that cameramen had gone down to the scene of the rioting and said to young blacks who were standing nervously on the sidewalk in front of some radio store: 'Get in, steal a television set, we want some action!' One only has to imagine how it would have been if there had been television cameras filming the storming of the Bastille. A new dimension of consciousness has been added to life by this invention. And all those young men wearing their hair long and with medallions

115

dangling from the chains round their necks seem perpetually ready improvisers of a performance which will last until they are thirty, that terminal moment of youth. They are less ashamed of publicity seeking than people were a generation ago. The result of regarding everything as an 'act' is that nothing is embarrassing.

Nevertheless the fact that in some ways they are different does not of itself constitute a 'generation gap'. In fact in America where, if there were such a gap, one would expect it to be widest, there is a good deal of evidence to show that journalists exaggerate it. Some of this evidence has been collected by Samuel Lubell (Director of the Opinion Reporting Workshop at Columbia University's School of Journalism). Among Mr Lubell's findings are:[1]

(1) much more continuity than gap exists between generations;
(2) parents have not been rendered obsolete but continue to exert an almost ineradicable influence on their children.

Amongst the results of interviews with students, Mr Lubell's team found that only one-tenth of the students interviewed differed greatly from their parents. Three-quarters would vote for the same political party as them. They did however find that in personal living the children were different, particularly with regard to drug habits, sex and in the weakening of their religious feelings.

Mr Lubell's general conclusion is that the 'really important challenge to the universities is coming, not from agitations for "student power", but from pressures originating outside the campus, which may necessitate a new relationship of the universities to our society'.

The briefest backward glance over events of the present century shows that people talk about a 'generation gap' when there are events happening in the society towards which members of different generations take up different attitudes. The greatest 'generation gap' existed during and immediately after the First

[1] Samuel Lubell, 'That Generation Gap', *The Public Interest*, 1968 (no. 13).

World War. This was not because generations had grown away from another but because the war formed as it were a wedge between them. The young had to fight in the war, the old stayed at home. There was less 'generation gap' in the Second World War, because in a war in which civilians were bombed there was not a great discrepancy between the risks undertaken between the younger generation and the older.

We would understand the young better if instead of thinking of a 'generation gap' we thought about things that go on in the society towards which young and old react differently. The society in which contemporaries live provides what might be termed a 'Production'. Young and old react to this in ways which are sometimes much the same, sometimes widely different. The point I want to make is that it is the 'Production' which produces the reactions, not some dramatic change in the continuity of generations. American slang is rich in synonyms for the 'Production'. It is sometimes called a Bandwagon, sometimes a Rat Race, perhaps it is the American Way of Life, or the American Dream even.

A few years ago – in spite of all those new inventions which were already with us – observers, if they remarked on the 'generation gap', did so to point out how narrow it was. Young men at college during the presidency of General Eisenhower, and for some time after, seemed only concerned with jumping on the bandwagon. Young Frenchmen, up to a matter of months ago, seemed anxious to do the same thing, to judge from a report based on answers to a questionnaire sent to 280,000 French boys and girls of ages between fifteen and twenty-four, and published in May 1967:[1]

The young French person dreams of marrying early, but takes precautions to avoid putting children into the world if means to raise them correctly are lacking. Also his objective No. 1 is success in his profession. While waiting for this he (or she) economises, he to buy a car, she to put together her trousseau. He interests himself in the problems of the hour, but does not ask to enter earlier into political life; 72 per cent of the young think that the right to vote should not be lowered from below the present age of 21. The young

[1] Philippe Labro et l'Equipe d'Edition Spéciale, *Ce n'est qu'un Début*, Paris (distributed by Editions Denoel). The extract cited here is from the *Livre Blanc de la Jeunesse*.

French person does not believe that there will soon be war and he thinks that the future will depend above all on industrial efficiency, internal order and the cohesion of the population.

Probably a majority of French of all ages – those who on the evening of de Gaulle's speech announcing new elections drove claxoning down the boulevards – do still believe all this, as perhaps a majority of students at Columbia believe corresponding things. However, a vociferous minority do not, and in rebellion it is the minorities that count.

The change is not due to a sudden widening of the 'generation gap' but to the felt presence in the society of stupefying things suddenly becoming intolerable. Today these are called Vietnam, but probably that name is a symbol for a great many other weighty, morally repellent obstructions including the whole intractable machinery of government itself, which has resulted in leadership in countries on both sides of the once-called Iron Curtain becoming representative of interests and bureaucracies which seem immovable. The old generation is found, for the most part, on one side of these objects or events, the young on the other. The old see above all the reasons why nothing can be done.

One can only compare what seems, to the militant students, to have happened in the external world of the society in which they live, to a kind of crystallisation, like the surface of a pond suddenly freezing and becoming covered with ice. They feel their inner world of personal values to be frozen over by the events taking place in the external public world of politics. The external world seems to threaten actually to disrupt the values of the inner world. To realise and even to retain his own values the student has to convert the most personal values of his own being into political counteraction. The non-political finds himself in a world where suddenly everything is explained in terms of politics.

When this happens the student appears in the eyes of his elders to have changed, and to become another person – with his odious Midas touch which turns everything to politics.

It is in such a situation that the kind of controversy occurs which is to be seen in a book called *Democracy and the Student Left*, which consists of an essay of that name by George Kennan, followed by replies from students and teachers. To understand the confrontation, you must think of Mr Kennan standing like an antique Roman, quite the noblest of them all, on one side of that institution, Princeton University, and today's militant students standing on the other. The institution has been a good deal altered by the fact that the student population has been multiplied perhaps tenfold since Mr Kennan's day and that there are a great many disturbances blowing like a typhoon through the campus. So Mr Kennan from his side of time sees a quite different university from that which the students see from theirs. To Mr Kennan the university is a place where 'there is a certain detachment and seclusion, a certain voluntary withdrawal and renunciation of participation in contemporary life in the interests of a better perspective on that life when the period of withdrawal is over'. It is brooded over by the ghost of another antique Roman, Woodrow Wilson, from whom Mr Kennan quotes, with austere fervour:[1]

I have had sight of the perfect place of learning in my thought: a free place, and a various, where no man could be and not know with how great a destiny knowledge had come into the world; but not perplexed, living with a singleness of aim not known without; the home of sagacious men, hardheaded and with a will to know, debaters of the world's questions every day and used to the rough ways of democracy; and yet a place removed – calm Science seated there, recluse, ascetic like a nun; not knowing that the world passes, not caring, if the truth but come in answer to her prayer. . . . A place where to hear the truth about the past and hold debate about the affairs of the present, with knowledge and without passion. . . .

etc., etc., it goes on like this. Doubtless to the militant students at Columbia, it would sound like a description of a nun ripe for raping.

As a good many correspondents pointed out, the demands on today's students implicit in Mr Kennan's description would have had more weight had they not been addressed to students many of whom had little chance of voluntary withdrawal. For hanging over them was the threat of being drafted to take part in the war in Vietnam. But Mr Kennan says they exaggerate the extent of this threat.

Mr Kennan goes on to criticise the militant students for

[1] George F. Kennan, *Democracy and the Student Left*, Boston (Atlantic/Little Brown), London (Hutchinson) 1968.

their ignorance and he objects to the destructive violence of their protests. He thinks that if the young find the political structure objectionable they should 'put forward a programme of constitutional amendment or political reform' and promote it 'with reasoned argument and discussion', instead of their having no programme and indulging in 'violence for violence's sake' and 'in attempts to frighten or intimidate an administration into doing things for which it can itself see neither the rational nor the electoral mandate'. Mr Kennan also takes exception to those who protest by violating the law, even though they are prepared to accept the legal consequences of doing so.

Mr Kennan invites the young to try and change the constitution before protesting about Vietnam. This seems like asking them to wait a very long time before acting about something of the most immediate urgency.

The volume contains a great many answers – some of them abusive – to Mr Kennan. One of the best is a polite and well reasoned letter written with a courtesy and distinction almost the equal of Mr Kennan's own, by David King, a Harvard freshman. He regards Mr Kennan as 'the personification of the balance between idealism and realism that I would like, eventually, to attain'. Nevertheless he disagrees profoundly with him. His letter goes to show, I think, that it is not a change in the mentality of generations that has caused the division between old and young but a situation which has put the old on the side of what the young regard as immorality, the young on the side of what the old see correctly as rebellion. Mr King declares that he is not against the draft, which he regards as an odious necessity, but nevertheless he supports those who consider that when it involves their being sent to Vietnam the draft 'constitutes a violation of their personal morality'. He compares the draft to a tax applied to raise not money but manpower for 'enforcing the policies of the government'.[1]

In this situation the law is reaching into the personal domain of a man's soul. . . . In the end, every individual is responsible to a higher authority than the government and whether it is religious or

[1] George F. Kennan, *Democracy and the Student Left*, Boston (Atlantic/Little Brown).

personal it is sacrosanct. The United States itself held this view in the Nuremberg trials when it found that 'following orders' does not excuse one from the consequences of his actions.

He considers that one is justified in 'resisting the government's attempt to subvert his morals'.

Partly I have given this example to show that a young student who is not a Hippie, or an *enragé*, may nevertheless feel that what a much respected member of the older generation considers political complexity, he considers moral outrage. Mr King finds American policy so immoral that he compares it with the actions for which Nazi leaders were tried at Nuremberg. And what this quiet-mannered freshman who so admires Mr Kennan asks for is the politics of a different morality. In asking this, Mr King is of course attempting to reduce immensely tangled political problems to simple either/or propositions. One can sympathise with Mr Kennan writing:[1]

Never has there been an era when the problems of public policy even approached in their complexity those by which our society is confronted today, in this age of technical innovation and the explosion of knowledge. The understanding of these problems is something to which one could well give years of disciplined and restrained study, years of the scholar's detachment, years of readiness to reserve judgement while evidence is being accumulated. And this being so, one is struck to see such massive certainties already present in the minds of people who not only *have not* studied very much but presumably *are not* studying a great deal because it is hard to imagine that the activities to which this aroused portion of our student population gives itself are ones readily compatible with quiet and successful study.

Yet if the students whom Mr Kennan addresses oversimplify issues Mr Kennan does the reverse. Or perhaps Mr Kennan, with all his subtlety is *not*, after all, complex enough. For what he fails to see is that complex though an international problem such as the position of America in Asia may be, war itself is a simplification. I may have immensely complex reasons for hating my neighbour and grievances against him which anyone who devoted ten years to studying the matter would admit to be just, but if I murder him I have

[1] George F. Kennan, *Democracy and the Student Left*, Boston (Atlantic/Little Brown).

121

simplified the issue to the method and fact of murder, and although study of the complex situation might mitigate the offence, I have murdered just the same.

I know that this answer is not conclusive, unless for a pacifist, because we do not in all circumstances condemn war, but it goes a long way. Napalm bombs iron out the complexities of politics. Even if going to war is accepted as a 'necessary crime' the fighting can, if protracted, and the methods used can, if excessively horrible, render the decision to fight a mistake. This is especially true, I think, of colonial wars which are usually 'interventions' by an external power in a civil war, rather than direct invasions. The intervention ceases to be justified – just as colonialism – and the colonialist – ceases to be justified if too many people on the spot do not want the intervener, or if the side against which he intervenes resists for an indefinite period. I agree that the whole history of colonial wars goes to show that intervention is an immensely complicated strategic and political operation. But these complexities do not invalidate the position of a person who simply thinks that intervention is wrong; nor of one who comes to think that the operation by its extent and horror has been proved to be wrong. There is virtue of course in knowing as much as possible about the complexities of the situation – it is admirable to do so – but the person who objects on moral grounds is not answered by saying that he knows too little about it.

These observations, I know, breed further complexities. It will be argued that if the Americans were not in Vietnam, the Chinese or the Russians or the local Communists would be there and in neighbouring parts of south-east Asia. The arguments are certainly very involved but here again, given the methods used or excused, there is a clash between considerations of complex strategy and those of simple morality. If someone considers that it is morally wrong to defend one position because of the hypothetical possibility of failure to defend it leading to the loss of other positions, and he refuses to enter into complicated studies and calculations about the wrong, there is not much point in rebuking him for ignoring complexities.

But it is true that unless a conflict between morals and policy had arisen, there would be no question of such simplification. The student would be studying, playing games or writing a poem.

Mr Kennan, who is civilised, intelligent and Christian, nevertheless seems almost congenitally disposed to think that if there is a conflict between a hypothetically correct (because 'realistic') policy and a moral one, the first is bound to be right and the second wrong. He produces against the students who object, perhaps over-officiously, to universities having investments in South Africa, the following *témoignage*:[1]

I myself recently spent some time in South Africa, and I know of no one familiar with the situation there who does not see in the continued rapid development of the South African economy the greatest single impediment to the realisation of the official concept of *apartheid* and the greatest hope, accordingly, for advancement of the country's black and 'coloured' inhabitants. It is further evident that every intensification of the isolation of that country from the world community plays into the hands of the regime in its efforts to impose the policies of 'separate development'. Whoever is sincerely interested in the breakdown of the existing racial restrictions there ought normally to be interested in encouraging both the development of South African industry as such and the maximum participation of foreign capital in the process.

I feel that Mr Kennan ought not to have advanced this argument without mentioning the names of some of the people he did – and did not – meet (how many blacks, for example) in South Africa. Not to have done so lays him open to reminder that there were people who went to Germany in the mid-Thirties and who were very willing to produce similar bland arguments. They came back saying that all the businessmen they met assured them that nothing would help the Jews more than support for the German economy. They may have been right and Mr Kennan may be right but the note of bland assurance is not really quite all it pretends to be: good sense and the consensus of everyone met who is open to reason.

Mr Kennan does not answer the point implicitly made in Mr King's words about 'the law reaching into the domain of a man's soul' – that the 'draft resister is resisting the government's attempts to subvert his morals' – unless he does so by drawing

[1] George F. Kennan, *Democracy and the Student Left*, Boston (Atlantic/Little Brown).

attention to the fact that the whole thing is greatly exaggerated –
very few students are going to be drafted anyway. But Mr
Kennan and Mr King are really at cross purposes. Mr Kennan's
basic assumption is that if the students had really studied the
matters under discussion they would not protest or burn their
draft cards. After years of study they would undertake a long-
term operation to alter the American constitution. Mr King's
position is that the war is wicked and should be resisted by
every possible means, legal or illegal.

The point I am concerned with making is that on one level,
that of politeness, there is no quarrel between Mr King and
Mr Kennan. On another level, that of political tactics versus
morality, there is total disagreement. Politeness may not seem
of major importance here, but it is symptomatic. Mr King's
letter is the exception that proves the rule of the students' tone
which is one of studied rudeness, insolence and boorishness.
The reason for this is that most students evidently no longer
think they are addressing the authorities as 'persons'. If they
address them as such, they do so jeeringly, mockingly, striking
a note of false conviviality, as though both parties, the insulter
and the insulted, should agree that the older man only pretends
to be a person. He is really inhuman authority incarnate. The
political leaders, college presidents, etc., tend to disappear into
patterns of power and governmental or business interest – the
realities behind the carnival masks (Nixon and Humphrey)
which grotesquely caricature the human. On the other hand, if
someone appears on the public stage who has claims to be
human – for example, Senator McCarthy – he is immensely
welcomed and supported by some students, while others – the
more radical – try to prove that his human look is just as much
a pretence as that of the others. They take off the mask of the
real personality to show that of the false personality behind.

Thus the situation that Mr Kennan and his critics demonstrate is one of complex politics confronted by simplicist
morality. Somewhere between the two, the democracy, if not
the forms to which Mr Kennan attaches a justifiable importance,
is endangered. For if there are reasons so complicated that they
cannot be explained to people to justify the politics that the
most intelligent and thoughtful of the young find immoral,
then politics becomes a mystery which can only be played by

the most powerful and astute, and only understood by the most learned. This makes democratic processes irrelevant and mischievous, the intrusion of ignorant people into the affairs of knowledgeable ones. But if the government of a democracy is so wicked that the young are justified in disregarding its processes and refusing to obey its laws, then democracy will go by the board before some form of revolution, probably leading first to anarchy and next to dictatorship.

This is the situation, in which, on the one hand there seems to be nothing but unscrupulous power politics, on the other, no choice but revolution in the name of morals.

The Situation of Young Rebels

The Pattern of Cynicism

The breakdown of communication between generations, which has contributed to the militancy of the students, is the result of a particular kind of situation. This situation is liable to occur when a government, the ruling class, or/and the political establishment acts in a way which seems to the young a violation or betrayal of ideals. By 'ideals' here I do not mean anything very rarefied and exalted or even anything peculiar to the young. Ideals usually derive from ideas of behaviour absorbed from the atmosphere, so to speak, during childhood and youth. In America, presumably children have absorbed some idea of liberty and of the Rights of Man. In England they certainly acquire concepts of freedom for which traditionally the British are ready to fight: they also acquire a sense of justice and fair play. The French certainly inherit an ideal of critical intelligence and revolutionary ideals, as well as traditional ones. The criticism of the old by the young in politics is in the last analysis that the old have betrayed the ideals which they themselves taught the young. In the revolutionary postures of the young there is a strange mixture of conservatism.

The writers of the Cox Commission Report, *Crisis at Columbia* bear this out when they write:[1]

As one student observed during our investigation, today's students take seriously the ideals taught in schools and churches, and often at home, and then they see a system that denies its ideals in its actual life. Racial injustice and the war in Vietnam stand out as prime illustrations of our society's deviation from its professed ideals and of the slowness with which the system reforms itself. That they seemingly can do so little to correct the wrongs through conventional political discourse tends to produce in the most idealistic and energetic students a strong sense of frustration.

[1] Cox Commission, *Crisis at Columbia* (*The Cox Commission Report*), New York (Random).

129

The American correspondent of a British newspaper wrote during the recent presidential elections that cynicism had become a national joke in America. With the young this results from cynicism about what they suppose to be the cynicism of their elders. Thus the young are cynical about the CIA recruiting for personnel on college campuses because they regard it as cynical. But the students themselves may be said to be cynical when they describe occupying university buildings as 'liberating' them. And having done so, to 'release' the president's suppressed letters (that is to say his personal correspondence) to demonstrate the involvement of the university with military and intelligence government organisations. Terms like 'liberate' and 'release' would be hypocritical if it was not evident that they were used ironically, and to show up the cynicism and hypocrisy of the authorities.

While being cynical about their elders, the young retain their own idealism. Even their most 'shocking' behaviour is idealistic, with this curious double-bluff of behaving outrageously in order to expose the cynicism and hypocrisy of those in authority. The Cox Report quotes a witness of the behaviour of the students occupying Fayerweather Hall during the Columbia uprising:[1]

People slept in classroom buildings and hallways. And always meetings and meetings lasting long into the night. Participatory democracy. There was a real community spirit; everything belonged to everybody; the building was 'liberated'. Girls – about 40 per cent – were not expected to do the kitchen work alone, for this was a 'liberated' area, and boys had to help. Couples slept together in public view, nobody cared, we were 'liberated': here was a single commune in which adult hypocrisies did not apply any longer, where people shared and shared alike, where democracy decided everything, where people were free of adult values and codes. Fayerweather was tense, 'up tight', but free and in high spirits.

Idealism is the reverse of cynicism, its opposite which it may easily become. Our realisation of this is shown in language: in the exhortation 'do not lose your ideals', which suggests that behind the young idealist there lurks a cynic waiting in the

[1] Cox Commission, *Crisis at Columbia* (*The Cox Commission Report*), New York (Random).

wings. Indeed a classical theme of French novels is exactly this: the young man, Julien Sorel or Lucien de Rubempré who is an idealist, a poet, loses his ideals when he comes to the city and realises that the life there is run on cynicism and the betrayal of ideals.

The young are often idealistic, but I do not want, on account of this to idealise youth. The young have their own kind of cynicism, but except when they are sharing in the cynicism of the old – which for them means cynicism *about* the old – about the university president, the liberals, the military – it is different from elderly cynicism. It is much more personal. A young man may be cynical in his attitude to parents or friends, or about sex, or about the way in which he exploits his charm to get on in life. But in all these things he seeks to add to his personality.

Young generations react to the impersonal cold cynicism of old ones by setting up their own idealism which attacks and rejects the old. At the same time they carry over into their politics the ideals that they consider the old to have betrayed.

Thus during the Thirties in England the anti-Fascists insisted on freedom of the individual to live and express himself as he chooses, the very English ideal which British governments had failed to support in their dealings with Nazi Germany.

And in May 1968 the French students lived for a few weeks the life of fraternity and equality which the paternalistic de Gaulle and the Gaullists with their passion for bourgeois property and privilege had, in their eyes, betrayed.

The American students at Columbia were fighting for a libertarian rather scruffy pioneering America in which everyone knows everyone else and says 'Hi!' which the vast impersonal machinery of the campus bureaucracy had, in their eyes, betrayed.

And the students of West Berlin were fighting for a Germany of ideals and pure theory which they felt the Germany of the economic miracle and of the grand coalition, blurring all distinction of ideas, had betrayed.

The *Oxford English Dictionary* definition of 'cynic' is 'one who shows a disposition to disbelieve in the sincerity or goodness of human motives and actions, and is wont to express this by sneers and sarcasms'.

Cynicism when it is the attitude of a government means treating people with contempt. This contempt may show itself in various ways: by the government deceiving people in ways that show it does not respect their wish to deal in truth; by its conducting policies high-handedly, so that those who criticise or oppose them are made to feel their powerlessness to do so; or by pursuing a policy which may receive the support of a majority but which nevertheless seems immoral to those who cherish the traditional ideals of the country.

An impression of cynicism may also be produced by the attitudes, the manners, even the age of the rulers. Gaullism seems paternalistic largely because the general is himself so old. Apart from questions of their physical and mental health, government by men of extremely advanced age results in polarities of distant superiority on the one side, fury and derision on the other. This was seen in the last years of Churchill's and of Adenauer's governments.

The cynicism of the old is not so much about persons (though of course the elderly cynic may carry on into later life many of the characteristics of the young one) as about things. It is the cynicism of those who accept that there is a machinery of society which is regardless of persons, ideals, feelings, and that you have to know how it works, move with its operations and not against them. 'This is how things work, you had better be with them. They will serve your interests, and they may even serve your principles in the end. But your ideals will work against both your interests and your principles, because they are not adapted to the operation of the machine which is called the world.' With all his high-mindedness, this is what Mr Kennan means when he tells us that the best way to advance the cause of the 'blacks' in South Africa is to support the economic interests of the present South African government. However there is something about such cynicism which reminds us of Lincoln's remark that you can't deceive all of the people all of the time. When the cynicism of a society becomes mechanical, then people who retain their human values become cynical about the society, and its leaders.

132

The CIA Example

During the Fifties and Sixties, the incursion of the Central Intelligence Agencies into youth organisations and intellectual life was an example of a cynical governmental operation. This is true, however defensible the motives may be of some of those who worked it (and I know one at least whom I am sure had good intentions).

The CIA secretly supported youth organisations, youth conferences, and through the Congress for Cultural Freedom, international meetings of various kinds, and several periodicals and other publications.

Many of these undertakings had results good in themselves. For example, in the early Fifties I attended a conference on the economics of free societies held in Milan, with Hugh Gaitskill, R. H. S. Crossman, Kenneth Galbraith, George Kennan and many other leading figures, which Gaitskill described to me as the most interesting meeting of the kind he had attended. Some of the magazines published important material. Wonderful international performances of music and theatre were arranged by the congress. The youth conferences and publications were good in their different ways.

However the fact remains that all but a small circle of organisers were deceived in general and lied to in particular as to the origins of the funds. A situation was built into the structures of the CIA-supported organisations which had the result that their personnel and their associates divided into three categories: (1) those agents and representatives of the CIA who knew exactly what the position was; (2) those close associates who did not know but who had the strongest suspicions; (3) those who did not know and who, if they made inquiries, received evasive or untruthful answers.

This is what I call a cynical pattern. For quite apart from the personal attitudes and motives of those in the first category, they were through their deception in fact *using* those in the third category, often people much their superiors. In using them, they were also misusing freedom by putting it at the service of political schemes which were concealed.

After the CIA penetration of cultural organisations had been exposed (first by the *New York Times* and later, in much more detail, by *Ramparts*) many people defended the CIA. They pointed out that during the Fifties the activities of Senator Joseph McCarthy and the Un-American Activities Committee made it impossible for the American government to sponsor intellectuals and students with liberal views and to send them to international meetings. The secret use of CIA funds had made it possible to do this. This argument does not alter the fact that those sent, who had in many cases been told that their expenses were being paid with Foundation money, were being manipulated. If they had been told who was paying for their presence, many of them would have refused to go.

Sometimes, as I was to find when I was co-editor of *Encounter*, a magazine sponsored by the Congress of Cultural Freedom, which channelled money for it supposedly from an organisation called the Farfield Foundation, one was directly lied to. After an article had appeared in the *New York Times* stating that *Encounter* was subsidised by CIA funds, indirectly funnelled, I wrote to the head of the Farfield Foundation to ask him if this was true. I received from him the most emphatic denial that there was any truth whatever in the charge.

It happened that before this I had gone to Mr Cecil King at the offices of the *Daily Mirror* and asked him to take over support for *Encounter*, which he generously agreed to do. However even after *Encounter* received this support, questions arose as to its past, as a result of the publicity given by the *New York Times*. At a meeting of the International Pen Club in New York, Mr Conor Cruse O'Brien gave a lecture analysing the material of *Encounter* in the light of its support from the CIA. Mr Frank Kermode, who had succeeded me as co-editor (I became American corresponding editor), told the American editor that O'Brien's remarks, if untrue, were actionable. The American editor assured him that they were completely false. On the basis of this assurance when the editor of *New Statesman* told Frank Kermode, a few weeks later, that he had O'Brien's article in proof and was about to publish it, Frank Kermode replied that if he did so, *Encounter* would have to sue.

Later, however, it became clear that Kermode had been deceived by his American co-editor; that *Encounter* had indeed, previous to the *Daily Mirror* support, been subsidised by the CIA with money channelled through the Farfield Foundation.

Frank Kermode and I resigned. Our American co-editor, who alone was cognisant of the CIA support, did not resign. I mention this autobiographic episode because at Columbia it was one of the first things that the students asked me about. Again at the Sorbonne, American students raised the question of the CIA. That they did so shows a difference I think between the older generation of the establishment and their generation. For a great many establishment people took the view that *Encounter* had justified itself by its achievement, and that the question of where the money came from was unimportant. I did not agree with this, because in such an organisation if one member of an editorial board is privy to its support by secret governmental funds, concealing the fact from his colleagues, then, to the extent that he is manipulating them by using their reputations without their knowledge of the terms on which this is done, and in the service of an undisclosed interest, the contributors and readers are likewise being manipulated. The scandal was implicit in the pattern, which was cynical.

The rebellious young who knew very well the whole CIA affair and who themselves, through the involvement of the youth organisations, felt tainted by it, saw the CIA action as a model almost of what they called 'manipulation' which they regarded as one of the worst features of the society and the organisations against which they were fighting.

Romantics and Beatniks

The total opposition of the militant students to the older generation is the result of a situation in which, in the eyes of the young, the establishment appear not as human beings but as representatives of interest, privilege, things. This is symbolised for the young by Vietnam. But the situation is not new. It is reminiscent for example of the attitude of the English Romantics to the old regime at the time of the French Revolution.

With Church and State and their whole world threatened, George III and his ministers reacted by opposing the revolutionaries whether in Europe or America, and by crushing all signs of revolution at home. As a consequence the young Romantic poets identified the order of the kings and priests and reactionary rulers with pure evil, destruction and death:

> I met Murder on the way –
> He had a mask like Castlereagh –
> Very smooth he looked, yet grim;
> Seven blood-hounds followed him:
>
> All were fat; and well they might
> Be in admirable plight,
> For one by one, and two by two,
> He tossed them human hearts to chew
> which from his wide cloak he drew.

Any young American poet, reflecting on the bombing of North Vietnam, might write in similar vein of any American presidential candidate of the 1968 November election.

To the young Romantic poets of that time, the government which tried to crush forces of revolution at home and abroad seemed to be trying to destroy life itself. Perhaps the assertive, self-destroying lives of Byron, Keats and Shelley were an unconscious protest of a very personal kind against the society of the time, because the Romantics were by no means effective as politicians.

So the young Americans who hold revolutionary views visualise a struggle between everything that is inhuman in the American system and everything which they recognise as human in themselves. Those who govern, and whose interests influence government, those who conform in education and public relations, seem to them simply inhuman, dehumanised. They raise their voices hysterically in opposition to those who in the time and place of war calculate human lives and deaths with computers, in time and place of peace deal with people by the methods of public relations and advertising.

Just as the young poets of the Romantic movement responded to a Europe torn between revolution and reaction, first of all with impassioned cries torn out of their lives, so the original protest of rebelling young Americans against America was the Beatnik one of asserting hysterical rebellious identities against the mechanised dominating conformism of America. The Beatnik regarded himself as at once a rebel and a product of his time. 'The production' made him a rebel. He howled because he had been driven down but the howl is malicious and vengeful:

136

I saw the best minds of my generation destroyed by
    madness, starving hysterical naked,
dragging themselves through the negro streets at dawn
    looking for an angry fix,
angelheaded hipsters burning for the ancient heavenly
    connection to the starry dynamo in the
    machinery of night . . . .

This astral machinery is certainly that of late Romanticism.

The Beatniks were opposed to the values of money, clean-living and conformism. They were outrageous, deliberately and provocatively so, as though they had studied secrets of being scandalous from dark pages of the Old Testament. They were erudite in the possibilities of dishevelled hair, unkempt beards, defiant raggedness, madness, pads, rooms, food, sex and syringes, offensive to the right feeling, right-dressed conforming – educated or illiterate – citizen. There is a legend that, when he was young, Allen Ginsberg would dislocate a public argument with a 'square' opponent by undressing on the platform and challenging his opponent also to do the same.

Outrages of this kind parody public life – anticipating and sabotaging phenomena such as the Nixon-Kennedy debates on television.

The Beatniks, however, with their insistence on the values of the private paraded publicly, were against politics, which they regarded as 'square'. Nevertheless, their protest had political implications, even in deriding politics. It was in no sense escapist or a retreat into private life. They were the earliest generation of the young who learned to flaunt their private virtues and vices on the television screen.

In 1957 when I was giving some lectures at Berkeley, I got to know Allen Ginsberg. I was struck by the contrast between the gentle, forbearing, modest and attentive man who was the private Ginsberg, and the competitive publicity-seeking notorious Ginsberg. He was living in San Francisco at the time, and he would sometimes come over for an afternoon to Berkeley and spend hours talking quietly about poetry and his ideas – he had the faith in goodness of the religious mystic – without any sign of craving for an audience of more than one. I saw the other Ginsberg for the first time when I was asked to take part in a television discussion with him. We had no sooner got in

137

front of the camera than Ginsberg pushed me aside, stared with glowing eyes straight into the lens and started making a dithyrambic speech about the Beatniks, announcing some meeting which was to take place soon in San Francisco. At first I was rather shocked at this revelation of the Ginsberg who was conscious to excess of the value of plugs and commercials. Later I came to think that my reaction was an effect of my genteel English upbringing. For I thought of people as divided into public and private. And being a person who respected private values I had always been rather ashamed of the side of me which is public. But for Ginsberg and his friends, the Beatniks, the Hippies, the Yippies, the psychedelic generation, the private life, was simply the deepest rhythm of their public rhetoric directed against America.

Ten years later, meeting Ginsberg in New York in the spring of 1968, I thought the private and the public had come together in a resonant quietism. I wanted to discover his views about Columbia – where he had been a student – so I started trying to find him in New York. He was extremely inaccessible. When I at last did reach him he called at my hotel and we then walked together along the edge of Central Park. His very striking appearance and dress made him eminently recognisable, and he was indeed recognised – by almost everyone, I should say. With his rich locks hanging down to his shoulders as though plaited, his sumptuous beard, his shining black eyes staring straight ahead of him, in his long dhoti-like robe and with a carpet bag hanging over his shoulder, which he corrected from swinging to and fro with his left hand, he looked like a cross between a Hebrew prophet and a Hindu guru. He scarcely seemed ruffled by the exclamations of recognition which broke all round him – surf over a boat's prow – as he thrust steadily forward. His conversation was equally apocalyptic, as in quiet tones he explained that the American cities were bound to break down if only on account of air pollution by the increasing fumes of gasoline in the traffic-choked streets. It was as plain as daylight to him that the cities would achieve their own destruction and that there would be a revolution. Revolution was the answer to the problems of bare survival. If the cities were not choked in their own fumes, then they would in any case decay and become slums, be torn to pieces by racial riots, have bombs fall on them, which would destroy urban industrial America. He pronounced all this in a spirit of cheerful calm and drew the conclusion that protests made by students and others should not just be against the old America falling to pieces, they should be models of the new life of love and awareness. When the Hippies went on the protest march against Vietnam in Washington, thcy did not attack the military and the police, nor were they content to be completely passive, they stuck flowers in the soldier's gun barrels. He spoke of an occasion when the Red Devils (a motor cycle gang) decided to attack the Hippies. The Hippies debated whether they should arm themselves with clubs and chains, and decided instead to exercise the power of flowers, and to charm and seduce the Red Devils, a policy eminently successful.

As we walked along Broadway, a woman suddenly emerged from the moving sidewalk crowd, hurled herself at Ginsberg, threw her arms around him and gave him a series of tremendous hugs, punctuated by shouts of joy. Allen responded gently, disentangled himself and continued his conversation, observing in parenthesis: 'Lived with her seven years ago. The girl I was really hot for,' and he went on to describe a kind of communication which could be defined as either pre-verbal or beyond language. As an example of it there was the occasion when he had spoken in the summer of 1966 to a great crowd of students at Prague University (they had elected him King of the May and he had been forced by the authorities to leave Czechoslovakia after this). He had addressed them in a language they did not understand and yet he had entered into a direct communication with them which came from his whole body – rather than from the head, that repository of ideas which might well have been brainwashed. I asked him about the universities. He said that Academe meant a grove of trees where there should be taught not just knowledge but wisdom. Tibetan teachers should be made available at Columbia. Wisdom meant non-verbal non-conceptual sensory training in expansion of consciousness, teaching students to attain a state of awareness without the use of language. The great thing to avoid was brainwashing. Our education excelled in just that. There was a need for a psychic transformation. Political protest against social evils was not enough. What was required, even while the protest was going on, was to live according to 'new models of transitional action'.

Ginsberg is a latter-day prophet, an extraordinary but immediately recognisable phenomenon. The fact that just walking down the street he *was* recognised, by more people and with more delight, than, in an unannounced stroll, any presidential candidate would be – is encouraging and something to be grateful for. That the students of Prague, to whom his ideas may not have seemed particularly relevant to their problems, should have greeted him with acclaim is still better, for it points to the fact that on the level of goodness, eloquence, warmth and sincerity there might be understanding between those whose ideas differ but who agree in wanting a better world.

Ginsberg represents what may be new techniques of consciousness and communication (though it is arguable that they are very old) and he also represents an ancient wisdom. Essentially he believes in the truth: by which I do not mean scientific truth but, rather, a truth which everyone recognises and which only has to be spoken – or which need not be spoken, only has to be in the present flesh – for it to be accepted. Even when the truth becomes separated from authoritative religion universally accepted (as in biblical Israel) it remains the truth. Without shared belief, however, perhaps the truth becomes separated from the Word, because people cannot agree on a common formula of revelation. This may be why Ginsberg insists so on the pre-verbal truth, that which rests in an almost preconscious awareness that people share a common life, that of the flesh and goodness and dream.

The Beatniks had the international influence of their style and their vocabulary which was obscene, and their eloquence which was uninhibited and sustained like the outpourings of the surrealists from the subconscious but with a much more obvious rhetoric. It was the assertion of their souls and their bodies against the non-soul non-body of the great American machine. It had the inspiration of some sustained fit of oaths from the mouth of a drunken Welshman (it would hardly have been possible without Dylan Thomas) or a kilted Scot. The style reached as far as the night clubs of Warsaw with their guitar playing youths reciting songs of all the civil wars – Communist and Fascist – of the twentieth century. It was not only a fashion

140

that spread but an expression of youth defying the bureaucrats and propagandist leaders of the state with their hideous technetronic jargon.

It is often said that the Beatniks 'contracted out' of society and this is true in the sense that they could not possibly have formed a political party: they were candidates not for parliament but for prison, and as an opposition endlessly preoccupied with incriminating themselves, God's own gift to the police. They opted out of politics because politics meant the world of Congress, parliament, government, power, business, against which they had hurled down their gauntlet of beard, jeans, buckles, pads, dope and easy sex.

Yet if you regard the society in which you live as alien, there is only a step between contracting out and taking active measures to oppose it. That step is taken when you see the society not just as an agglomeration of elements, one of which is politics, but as the material result of politics. You may switch then from thinking that politics is nothing to thinking it is everything. Politics becomes a process which you can only reverse by an opposing politics.

Thus the successors of the Beatniks, the Hippies, on the Columbia campus and at the Chicago convention of the Democratic party, began with protests, sit-ins, flowers, and ended with the conviction that the police brutality used against them was part of the omnipresent politics. This development was inevitable because contracting out was to live in a vacuum. Contracting out was only possible when, like Jimmy Porter in *Look Back In Anger*, it was still possible to think that the great good causes of politics had all been exhausted in the Thirties.

The Situation of the Thirties

There are parallels between the generation of the Fifties and Sixties and that of the Thirties.

The Oxford and Cambridge students of the mid-Twenties were a non-political, indeed an anti-political, generation. They admired the writing of the postwar era – that of Forster, Eliot, Huxley, Lawrence, Hemingway, all of whom connected politics with the futility of the war and postwar era, catastrophes of

141

hunger and inflation. The revolutions in Russia and eastern Europe seemed like portents of the end of civilisation. The ineffectiveness of social idealism was demonstrated by the League of Nations.

Certain titles of books sum up a generation. *The Decline of the West* and *The Waste Land* did this for the Twenties.

So in Oxford and Cambridge and in London, the postwar mood was one of aestheticism tinted with a pink of socialism. If there were any politics they would have to be apocalyptic. Professional politics were the pattern of cynicism. In the early Thirties, undergraduates were divided into 'hearties' who played games, and aesthetes, who looked at, listened to, made art. The Oxford Union was a preserve for 'squares' who hoped to go into politics, not to change them.

The aesthetes were too effete to correspond to the far more lively American Beatniks and Hippies of today. All the same some of their attitudes were not dissimilar. They abhorred the values of the surrounding society. They led lives of studied self-fulfilment. They lacked, though, the evangelical, get-to-heaven-by-way-of-damnation tone of the hairy young Americans. They found the meaning of life in art and in personal relations.

And when, in the Thirties, young people corresponding to those who would have been aesthetes five years earlier turned to politics they did so, still hating public life and the whole establishment political scene.

It is interesting to recall that the idea of the revolution as something palpable, more than dream, accompanied the rise of Hitler some years before his seizure of power in February 1933. For the rise of Hitler in Germany, steep from 1929 on, was paralleled in Germany by the almost as equally steep growth of Communism. So if in 1930 one was twenty-one, Communism did not mean the Stalinism of the mid-Thirties at the time of the great trials. It meant, in Berlin, where I was much of my time, the revolution as projected by Eisenstein and the other great film directors of that time, and as written up by travellers to the Russian Revolution still in ferment. One did not think of the dictatorship of the proletariat but, rather, of *Ten Days that Shook the World, Potemkin, Earth, Mother,* and the same ideas of revolution reflected in the plays of expressionist dramatists like Ernst Toller and Georg Kaiser. This was the revolution of the early days and – subject for talk like that at the Sorbonne – visions of the revolution as it would be after the withering away of the state. To us in 1930 it seemed as Castro's Cuba seems to the young of today.

Political action became urgent when the Nazis had gained power, and sent Jews and intellectuals to prisons and camps, burned books, banned all freedom of expression, occupied the Rhineland, forced the *Anschluss* on to Austria, intervened, together with Fascist Italy, on Franco's side in Spain and helped destroy the Spanish Republic. The Nazis built up an immense miltary machine that threatened Europeans, and people beyond Europe, with the same destruction of all freedoms as had been visited on Germany. Politics now meant for us supporting the victims of Fascism, fighting for freedom of expression, taking the side of beleaguered Madrid and Barcelona, trying to stop the Second World War from happening. It meant choosing life instead of death, and life meant then writing the things one wanted to say, and trying perhaps to project one's spirit into the cells and camps to be present with the victims. (I do not mean that I personally did this, but there were people who did a great deal, and some of the most shining of them died.)

In England, anti-Fascism was a movement of young people, most of whom were from middle class homes. It found its expression in the word 'Spain' as the movement of today finds its expression in 'Vietnam'. In opposing Fascism abroad the young felt that they were taking on the task of defending freedom and human rights, which had been thrust on them as the result of the dereliction of principle of the old. It was the old men who made cynical arrangements with Hitler and Mussolini – the non-Intervention treaty which permitted the Germans and Italians to intervene in Spain.

So anti-Fascism was a war on three fronts, the Fascists, the young anti-Fascists, and the old – the men of Munich. The young felt that the old had betrayed the values of democracy, those of freedom. In their connivance at the persecution of Jews, the burning of books, the destruction of all free expression in the arts, the Baldwins, MacDonalds, Simons, Hoares, Lavals, were felt by the young to be cynical to the point of being inhuman. This judgment is of course an oversimplification. They were frightened men who belonged to the generation of the

143

so-called Great War against Germany, and they dreaded above everything else a repetition of the Western Front. The point is, though, that there was an alienation of generations. The old and the young became in one another's eyes, bogeys. To the old their children seemed wild, destructive, dangerous revolution-aries; to the young, the old seemed either dead, or else on the side of things dead. Above all they were afraid of life, and their England, the England of the last shows of the British Empire, of King George V's Jubilee, seemed a painted screen behind which there was a strangled corpse.

The political aspects of anti-Fascism have rather obscured the psychological character of the Thirties. It lies however on the surface of the literature of the time. The struggle is seen not just as a conflict between political forces, or even between good and evil, but between life and death. In the most representa-tive poetry of the time, that of W. H. Auden, the younger generation is shown as instinctual new life which the young have to learn to release in themselves against the forces of death. Gradually the process by which the young take the Freudian side of the uninhibiting senses becomes linked up with the Marxist movement of history. The anti-Fascist liberating historic forces are identified with life, Fascism with death.

The young are cast in a role which is that of life, not just youth, and there is something sacrificial as well as arrogant about it. They are life's answer to the failure of the old to have matured into a richer and fuller life, their collapse into neurosis, decrepitude, premature death. The older generation is identified with causes that are doomed: imperialism, public schools, sexual inhibition. But there is no particular virtue attached to being young. It happens merely that the young have attained their majority at a moment when there was a struggle between the forces of life and the forces of death.

As I have remarked above, the non-political intellectuals who became anti-Fascist carried over into their anti-Fascism their dislike of official politics. And yet at this time the Labour party in England opposed Fascism; while anti-Fascist writers like Julian Bell and John Cornford, and other writers of the Thirties, though prepared to work with the Labour party

144

remained outside it. Even George Orwell, who with reason accused the Communist-inclined intellectuals of irresponsibility, when he went to Spain supported the Trotskyite POUM and fought with an anarchist battalion on the Catalan front.

When he was editing *The God that Failed* R. H. S. Crossman asked me why it was that my friends and I supported the Communists during the Thirties rather than the Labour Party. The question is relevant to the students of today, in fact it is the same question as that which some students at Columbia asked me: 'Why, do you think, is there radicalisation?' There are several answers. One I have already given: that being the non-political driven on to politics we retained our hatred for the established parties, and preferred to choose extremist ones. Another may be that Fascism itself was so extreme that one felt extreme remedies to be the only reply to it.

However, more than this counted the fact that the whole political system in which we lived seemed to be collapsing. From this point of view the Nazis were only a sympton of the decay of Europe. And the British and French failure to resist the Nazis was a symptom of the collapse of faith in our own liberal democracy. The answer to both Nazism and the failure of democracy seemed to be revolution.

Revolution was at first the dream. But with the Spanish Civil War it became different: what mattered now was the means: the means of combatting Fascism, the means of saving the Russian Revolution which was threatened, the means of making more revolution. The means are the concern of experts, who know what they should be. They involve setting the dream aside (for the time being), doing what the scientists of the Cause say, preserving discipline. Discipline, as we came to know, meant above all never criticising the Soviet Union. A great scandal of the mid-Thirties was the little volume of candid observations about his visit to Russia, published by André Gide, *Retour de l'URSS*. Gide was attacked by the Communists and the *communisants* French intellectuals with the combined zeal of the Church pronouncing excommunication and a military dictator in the midst of war incinerating those scraps of truth that give comfort to the enemy. A similar but much less sensational affair was the rejection by the editor of the *New*

Statesman of articles by George Orwell criticising the liquidation of the Catalan anarchists of the POUM.

Communism still represented the revolution. It had not become petrified into that system where there is only material progress and where the means of a bureaucratic state have become inseparable from the ends. The means however were dictatorial and to accept Communism meant accepting them. As the Spanish Civil War continued the anti-Fascists became more and more caught up in the means of Communism which were imposed first on the International Brigade and finally on the Republican government itself. Anti-Fascism lost its original romantic individualistic flavour and became the Communist organised Popular Front. Radicalisation is the process of being swallowed up.

With some part of their consciousness the militant students of today realise that a previous revolutionary generation ended in Stalinism. They see the results in Russia and eastern Europe and the unhappy but conformist and bureaucratised satellite countries of eastern Europe. They refuse however to entertain the idea that their revolution could end in the rule of a dictator, in a bureaucratised police state. A great many of their ideas express this refusal. The French students claim that they have no leaders. The outstanding personalities of their movement insist that they are only mouthpieces of the other students. One of the meanings of the frequently used expression 'spontaneity' is actions which arise from the mass or from the 'bases' and which are merely promulgated and put into effect by those self-effacing loud-speakers, the student leaders. 'Direct democracy' means rejecting centralised leadership, government, parliament even.

The students are convinced that their revolution will not be like any other. In Paris or Berlin they will explain to you that the 'bases' will be democratic, that there will be no leaders, that the 'structures' will be different. They will cite Castro and Che and Mao to show that the revolution can be 'permanent' and continue evolving under leaders who are prepared to

146

discuss their policies with people they meet in the street. If one mentions that the French Revolution began with committees planning Utopias, orations, turbulent figures voicing their wish for anonymity, they reply that they are an unprecedented generation.

The Anarchist Revolutionaries

Claude Roy has drawn my attention to a little known history of the Russian Revolution by the anarchist Vaeévolod Mikhailovitch Eichenbaum – better known under his pseudonym Voline – which contains ideas remarkably close to those of the students of Nanterre and the Sorbonne. Some of them must, I think, have read it, though they would probably deny having done so. But the fact that the commune set up by the Russian sailors at Kronstadt is so often cited by them as a revolutionary example indicates that they have studied the Russian Revolution from the anarchist point of view.

Voline was born at Vornoeje in Russia in 1882. Both his parents were doctors, so he was brought up in an intellectual environment. He was a student at St Petersburg during the events of 1905, at which time he was a revolutionary socialist. He was imprisoned but escaped to France in 1907. He became friendly with anarchist Russian refugees and became himself an anarchist. He escaped internment in France during the first world war by going to America, where he also frequented Russian anarchist circles. In 1917 he went to Russia where he wrote for and edited various anarchist publications. He was arrested in 1919 by the Cheka, released in October 1920 and arrested again in December of that year, but released once more as the result of the intervention of foreign syndicalist delegates visiting Moscow to attend a congress of the Profintern. He returned to Paris where he assisted in the publication of the Anarchist Encyclopedia. During the Spanish Civil War he edited, in Paris, the review *L'Espagne anti-Fasciste*. During the Second World War he lived in Marseilles where he wrote *La Révolution Inconnue* (1917–1921),[1] an anarchist's view of the Russian Revolution.

[1] Published by Les Amis de Voline, Paris.

147

It is a work of passion and sincerity, written in the disinterested spirit of a man who wants to state the truth about events through which he has lived. It is also a tribute to heroic idealists, the anarchists, who were later completely liquidated by the Bolsheviks. He poses an urgent question in his preface: How to stop a revolution from leading to a new enslavement of the people? 'What conditions would permit a revolution to avoid this sad end?' he asks. Is such an end the result of a sort of fatality of history? Is it the result of errors which might have been, with foresight, avoided? In which case, is it possible to avoid these errors in the revolutions of the future?

A great deal of the book is history seen from the anarchist point of view interspersed with the author's comments and reminiscences (there are striking anecdotes and reportage). There is an important chapter: '*Les deux Idées de la Révolution*', in which Voline attempts to answer the question posed in his preface. He makes an important distinction between two ideas of revolution. One idea was that of the Bolsheviks:

to construct, on the ruins of the bourgeois state, a new Workers' state: to constitute a 'workers' and peasants' government' to set up the 'dictatorship of the proletariat'. The anarchist idea was to transform the economic and social bases of the society *without having resource to a political state, to a government, to a dictatorship* . . . that is, to achieve the Revolution and resolve its problems not by *political and state means*, but by those of a natural and free activity, *economic* and *social*, of the *associations of the workers themselves*, after the overthrow of the last capitalist government.

The Bolshevik revolution envisaged:

in order *to co-ordinate* action, a central political power, which would organise the life of the state so as to assist the government and its agents, in accordance with the directives proceeding from the 'centre'.

The anarchist conception required:

the definite abandonment of the political and state organisation; *direct* and *federalised* harmony and collaboration of economic, social, technical or other organisms (syndicates, co-operatives, and various other forms of associations), locally, regionally, nationally, but rationally: and so a centralisation . . . proceeding from the governmental centre to the periphery of its control; but with the *economy* and *technology*, according to real needs and interests, proceeding from the circumference to the centres, established in a manner both natural and logical, in accordance with concrete needs, without domination nor orders.

One further quotation will give an idea of the meaning of anarchism for Voline:

The master idea of anarchism is simple: no party, political or ideological group, which puts itself outside or above the masses of working people in order to 'govern' or 'guide' them, will ever succeed in *emancipating* them, even if it sincerely desires to do so. *Effective* emancipation can only be realised by an *activity which is direct, vast and independent of interests* of the workers *themselves*, grouped not under the banner of a political party or an ideological formation, but in their own *class organisms* (syndicates of production, committees of factories, co-operatives, and so on) on the basis of a concrete *action* and of *self-government, assisted* but not governed by the revolutionaries working *at the very heart*, and not *above* the mass of the professional, technical, defensive and other organs.

Voline gives examples – the chief of them being Kronstadt – of how on several occasions during the Russian Revolution workers took over factories or other installations and started running them themselves. He thinks that they did so very effectively. But the central government always regarded this as a threat to their authority, and crushed such initiatives.

One of these episodes of the revolution anticipates the events of May in France when the workers took over the factories.

At the end of 1917 two or three workers from the Nobel petroleum factory at Petrograd, approached the anarchist 'union' to announce that the factory had been abandoned by the proprietors and that the workers had decided to make it work by themselves as a collective. With this intent they approached the government, the Bolsheviks, and asked for their aid. In reply they were informed that unfortunately under present conditions it was not possible to help them; the government could not obtain for them either fuel or raw material, or orders from clients, or means of transport, or funds. Moreover the Commissariat of Works (*Commissariat du Travail*) informed the workers' committee at the factory that the government had decided to close the factory and other factories in a similar position (of which there were a good many) giving the workers three months' pay.

The workers were not at all satisfied with this reply and said that they wanted to keep the factory working. They informed the government that they were certain of success in doing so. The government categorically refused. Voline has a nice phrase for their answer in which they stated that they had to plan production as a whole and that if 'each factory acted according to its fantasy, inextricable chaos would result'. The government then proposed that there should be a meeting at the factory where its representatives would put their point of view to the workers. It was as a result of this proposal, which the workers accepted, that the anarchists were asked, by two or three of them, to send an orator. Voline was sent as their representative. He describes vividly this meeting in a huge workshop, where the majority of the workers from the factory were assembled, a grave and reserved gathering with the members of the factory committee at a table, awaiting the government representatives. They arrived, very official, very serious, three or four of them, Chiliapnikoff himself, then *'Commissaire du Peuple au Travail'* at their head.

Chiliapnikoff spoke first. In dry, official tones he repeated the government's reply and the reasons for it and declared that it was irrevocable. This discourse was received in glacial silence.

Voline then made a speech in which he told the workers that they had the right to continue their work and that it was the duty of the government to give them every assistance in this task. The government should be encouraging instead of discouraging them. He then asked the workers whether they had the resources to carry out their work. He asked them whether they could divide themselves into little groups each of which specialised in problems of obtaining fuel, raw materials, etc. He then declared that if they could answer these questions satisfactorily, then

we the anarchists are sure that the workers themselves, having relations which reach everywhere all over the country, and knowing the essential elements of their work will know how to resolve their problems much more rapidly and simply than the government. We consider that to do this you have only to create mobile organisms of men capable, by their relationships, their understanding and their aptitudes, of acting energetically and with success. When their

150

mission is completed, these organisms will cease to exist and their members will rejoin the mass of the workers in the factory.

His speech, according to Voline, was enthusiastically received and the workers came forward with comments which showed that they very well understood what was expected of them. Voline then asked them, laughingly, not to form groups for the purpose of exploiting their fellow workers. They laughed. One after another workers declared that the whole undertaking would be in a spirit of comradeship. Voline declares that as a result of this discussion, the torpor with which the meeting had begun was dissipated.

Chiliapnikoff announced that nothing that had been said in any way affected the government's decision, and a few weeks later the factory was closed.

The Sabbath Made for Students

The workers at this Petrograd factory, with their little groups, each a specialist in some function of the work and yet all co-operating harmoniously, with their representatives sent out as emissaries into the wider world but reabsorbed into the mass of workers on their return, provide an example of the kind of society that the students at the Nanterre and the Sorbonne would like. When they look to the Red Guards of Mao's China and the Cuban Revolution of Castro and Che Guevara, it is in the belief, or the hope, that these revolutions are continually self-renewing in the manner of the Petrograd factory or the commune – the independent Soviet – of the sailors at Kronstadt, which was liquidated by the Bolsheviks.

The students are criticised for being influenced by anarchist theories and experiments, which are held to have failed or been discredited, or which, like Castro's revolution in Cuba, seem to have little relevance to the circumstances of any possible revolution in the west. They are criticised for the retrogressiveness of their theories which go back to the ideas of Proudhon, Fourier, Bakunin, Kropotkin and Sorel; perhaps further, to Godwin and his son-in-law Shelley, to the young Coleridge with his dream of colonising an island with settlers who would found the perfectly just society, with groups of early American

151

settlers who actually did make such experiments in social equality, cooperation, spontaneity and sexual freedom. One has to accept the force of George Kennan's accusation that they are simplicists who have not analysed the complexities of immensely tangled problems. Raymond Aron in *La Révolution Introuvable* sums up the objections in their most damaging form:[1]

In my view, they have fallen into the worst forms of utopianism or revolutionary mythology. More sympathetic than the communists, they are their intellectual inferiors. Let them read again some of the political philosophers who count in the history of western thought: Aristotle, Machiavelli, Hobbes, Spinoza, Hegel, Auguste Comte, Marx, and they will become convinced of this. The state of nature, during a few days of revolutionary carnival, does not lack charm. Very soon it becomes more insupportable than any other kind of order whatever. The student commune at the Sorbonne, at the end of several weeks, has given additional evidence of this.

Aron's argument has to be met if the militant students are to avoid supporting ideas and methods which could only lead to a worse state than the one against which they are revolting. But if he means that having read Aristotle and the rest they will see that they are mistaken, one may doubt that they need reach his conclusions any more than they would those of George Kennan. For with all his knowledge and distinguished brilliance Raymond Aron arrives at a sceptical conservatism which is not extraordinary. Ultimately political views that have force have to be simplified, though they should certainly be strengthened with knowledge. Simplification precedes study and, unless the reader is entangled in his knowledge, simplicity follows it. Aron has no real reason to assume that if they read these texts they would change their minds. George Kennan perceives this when he reflects that after all people's political views depend, finally, on their temperament. And he divides people into those who prefer social justice to order and those who prefer order to social justice. Kennan, like Aron, thinks order more important than social justice.

The difference between Aron and Kennan and the students is the old one of the difference between those who believe in the goodness of human nature and those who believe that, in all

[1] Raymond Aron, *La Révolution Introuvable*, Paris (Fayard) 1968.

circumstances, men are activated by the same bad motives and have the same bad nature, so that the best political system is that which disciplines and restrains them, and imposes 'order' on them. The militant students hold the opposite view that the full potentialities of human beings for good are not realised on account of the oppressiveness of the 'system'. In education and in society they look for uninhibited patterns of behaviour and 'spontaneity' which they hold will release the energies that they call the 'revolution'.

They might be wrong in all their ideas and yet justified in rebelling against the existing society. Their revolution might be doomed to failure and impossible of success, and yet it might have the inevitability of life, as it would, say if it were in opposition to the technetronic society which Zbigniev Brezezinski anticipates, a society in which complete information about everyone would be accessible to a central authority while at the same time everyone would be totally subject to brainwashing by propaganda. In such a society one could hardly be alive without being a rebel; but at the same time revolution would be impossible. The order which Raymond Aron and George Kennan prefer to disorder would then be simply the order of spiritual death. One is paying a compliment to M. Aron and Mr Kennan to say that in Brezezinski's society they might find themselves rebels.

The idea of the technetronic society seems to be under the auspices of Zbigniev Brezezinski, until recently a member of the Policy Planning Staff of the State Department, and now Director of the Research Institute on Communist Affairs at Columbia University. The 'technetronic society' seems to be the exact opposite of the society of 'spontaneity' demanded by revolutionary students, whom Mr Brezezinski evidently regards as pathetic throw-backs, survivors of Romantic days, forlornly playing out their anachronistic roles:[1]

Our society is leaving the phase of spontaneity and is entering a more self-conscious stage; ceasing to be an industrial society, it is being shaped to an ever-increasing extent by technology and electronics,

[1] *New Republic*, 13 December 1967.

and thus becoming the first *technetronic society*. This is at least in part the cause for much of the current tensions and violence, and largely the reason why events in America today do not fit established categories of analysis.

Mr Brezezinski realises that the technetronic society fills some people with uneasiness (in this respect the reactionaries and the revolutionaries are as one). 'The challenge in its essence involves the twin dangers of fragmentation and excessive control. A few examples: Symptoms of depersonalisation and alienation are easy to find. Many Americans feel "less free". This feeling seems connected with their loss of "purpose", for freedom implies loss of action, and action requires an awareness of goals.'

However Mr Brezezinski does not expect that the Luddite lovers of freedom and anarchy will seriously obstruct the new order. For one thing, 'it will soon be possible to assert almost continuous surveillance over every citizen and maintain up-to-date, complete files, containing even personal information about the health and personal behaviour of the citizen, in addition to the more customary data'. Moreover it will be possible to anticipate and plan to meet any uprisings in the future. The police will even be able to forecast crises before the rioters themselves are conscious of wanting them. Finally, over the hump, there may be a come-back for the romantics. Because if computers and information increase centralisation, they can also make possible decentralisation. If this is any comfort, the far-flung agent will have much greater freedom of action which can instantly be coordinated with the centre: the freedom of the spy and the roving cop who have initiative.

This glance into the computer-controlled future shows how difficult it is to distinguish between a revolutionary and a romantic reactionary today. One might even suggest that the prospect of a society in which bureaucratic leaders control the people much as meteorologists hope one day to control the weather, is a prospect against which the students are rebelling.

It is significant, surely, that the majority of works of science fiction published today foresee worlds which to people who are consciously aware of values of freedom are simply intolerable. One need not pretend that science fiction is an important branch of literature to suspect that the pessimism of this vast contemporary literature of anti-Utopias shows deep misgiving about the future of human consciousness.

What is most significant about the students' revolution is that it is directed against all existing forms of industrial society. The students do not like the western democracies, they do not like the People's Democracies of eastern Europe and they are suspicious of Czechoslovakia, which offered the prospect of a society combining Communism with the utmost possible individual freedom. The societies which they look to – China and Cuba – combine Communism with a backwardness of industrial development which admits of experiments in production like those which Voline describes in the factory at Petrograd. The social patterns they look to are anarchist theories and experiments of the nineteenth century and of the chaotic early stages of certain modern revolutions. Essentially what they object to are the standards and forms of organisation of modern industrial and technological societies.

Their protest is against a society whose standards and behaviour are determined by the exigencies of industrial planning, the domination of the rule of *things*. This began in England with the Industrial Revolution at the end of the eighteenth century when the agricultural workers were taken out of the villages and countryside and put into the barracks of the industrial slums. Goldsmith in *The Deserted Village* protested against the despoliation of rural life, Blake cried out against the 'dark satanic mills' of the industrial towns, Ruskin and William Morris wanted a modern socialism which returned to guilds and ancient communities, Dickens and even Tennyson lampooned the hard-faced industrialists, the profiteers and exploiters who were to become the new rich and the new aristocrats of the Victorian era.

And as the Industrial Revolution spread over Europe, men of intellect and imagination reacted with the same horror. Hoelderlin and Nietzsche, Baudelaire and Rimbaud, were insane with rage against the modern world of the bourgeois and the machine.

Sometimes the protestors looked back nostalgically to a Europe of an earlier time, before the Industrial Revolution. Sometimes they looked forward to a socialist or utopian future – the kind of world which came to be known as Wellsian – in

155

which there would be greater justice and an enlightened government and public. All of them – reactionary or rebellious –
despaired of religious or traditional values influencing contemporary society. Therefore either they looked back nostalgically
to a classical or religious past, or they looked forward to a
revolutionary future in which society would be used to create
a juster society of material welfare and of aesthetic values.
Whether they looked backward or forward was ultimately a
matter of the temperament – reactionary or rebellious, pessi-
mistic or optimistic – of the engaged.

Any vision of the future must admit the profound ambiguity
of science which can either create or destroy. It offers on the
one hand the means to wipe out all the achievements of civilisation, and on the other hand a future of greater prosperity and
material happiness than the world has ever known. Those who
have confidence in the scientific future are, on the whole, those
who have faith in human nature. For the technological world
makes past values anachronistic, and, since in itself it is as
neutral as nature, one has to have faith in the creative and
constructive qualities of human beings to believe that the future
will develop the creative rather than the destructive potentialities
of science.

So on the level of imagination and critical intelligence,
that is to say, where he applies these central faculties in himself
to the central activities of the time, where he is most penetrating,
the modern writer has little confidence in the values of modern
materialism. Whenever he has based his politics on the logic
of his imagination or his critical insight, he has found himself a
revolutionary, like Blake, Shelley or Rimbaud, or a reactionary
like Baudelaire, Nietzsche, Yeats, Pound or Eliot.

Occasionally, when events have seemed to confront writers
with the necessity of having to make an external political
choice corresponding to the inner choice they have already
made, they have shown their true sympathies, as they did in
the Thirties when so many young poets were revolutionary
socialists, while the older ones were Fascists. And at that time,
instinctively, they recognised that each had taken up his position
from the refusal to accept the values of industrial civilisation,
so that where there should have been bitter emnity between the
poets of the extreme left and those of the extreme right, there

was only a lovers' quarrel. In some famous lapidary lines the greatest modern poet (who happened to be a Fascist) summed up the attitude of revolutionary and reactionary:

Things fall apart; the centre cannot hold;
Mere anarchy is loosed upon the world,
The blood-dimmed tide is loosed, and everywhere
The ceremony of innocence is drowned.

This is a statement that strikes from the centre of the imagination to the centre of modern life. One would not have to search very far into the work of any poet since Blake and Shelley, including the Victorians, Tennyson, Browning and Arnold, to find parallel denunciation.

If in their actual lives most artists – unless driven to say what they really feel – have adopted the attitudes of an Aron or a Kennan and agreed that the preservation of the present set-up is better than to overthrow it, this is because they recognise that this materialist part-socialist part-capitalist democracy, with its leaders who are stewards of the great machines of mass production, does provide a margin of free-dom of movement and expression within which it is possible for body and mind to move with comfort. It is a margin which is constantly threatened with invasion by the political policemen of the central authority.

One can see today that what has happened in Czecho-slovakia might happen in other countries with the removal of marginal freedoms. In a technological society it is possible that the future of freedom will be confined to a few untouched sanctuaries. For this reason the students are to be feared as waking all the sleeping dogs of the police states. But the imagina-tion has known for a hundred and fifty years what their protest is about.

The students who criticise the consumer society feel that they live in a world which moves according to laws of the development of massive impersonal interests and technological invention of which they have no grasp. By grasp here I mean imaginative grasp, because they can of course analyse the system and theorise about it. Yet, except in so far as it impartially produces commodities of utility or destruction, they cannot relate it to their own lives. They cannot, to use the psychological jargon, *identify* with it, and probably the managers and operators of the machinery and economy of production seem to them as impersonal as the machines are inhuman.

This feeling of young people that they cannot identify these things that most passionately concern them with the motivations which seem most powerful in the surrounding society, is connected with another feeling of which they often complain: their failure to 'communicate'. By lack of communication they mean that they share no common language with those who in their words and ideas reflect the depersonalised interests of power. Lack of communication is felt as lack of freedom.

They do not and cannot mean – though they are often represented as doing so – that they lack freedom because their demands are not instantly complied with by a majority of people who may be opposed to them. What they mean is that they live in a society whose interests are of a scale which they cannot relate to their own scale of personal values. They are 'free' to speak in their private voices to public ears which cannot possibly be attuned to the sounds that they say. The question of their being free to realise their demands simply does not arise, because, not being powerful, they are not listened to. They think of the public world as being at the opposite extreme of Pascal's image of the heart that has its reasons that do not know reason. Their world has its reasons that do not know the heart.

Ever since the Industrial Revolution it has been impossible for the individual to envisage the organisational centre of productivity as being the extension of the inner world of values that are at once personal and generally human. Living in the modern world he can endow relationships and activities, art and sport, with traditional values, but when he approaches the main centres of the society he cannot project into them his imaginative life, because they do not embody values of living. They simply create market values. And yet they are the most important and central activities in our society, on which the survival of civilisation has been made to depend.

In the technological society, then, personal and traditional values are marginal. If to some extent they are still observed by those in power, then power itself mocks at them as mere empty form. Although technology may be useful, necessary and inevitable, in two important ways the imagination cannot grasp this. First, the individual in an industrial society cannot identify his own situation with that of the centres of power, except perhaps in very special situations such as that of the invasion of the nation by a foreign country, in which case the leaders become symbols for the nation's whole history, for the dead as well as for the living.

Secondly, and partly as a result of this lack of identification of the personal with the public world, the great interests connected with productivity do not provide models malleable to the imagination. In the pre-industrial societies it is clear that imagination provided the symbols of power. In the industrial society such symbols are aspects of public relations, advertising, selling things to a gullible public.

It is sometimes argued that the scientist is just as imaginative as the artist because the scientist also is a creator, and his flashes of inspiration resemble those with which the artist suddenly sees some new formula of words or paint or sounds which relates to one another experiences which have previously been disparate. This, I am sure, is true, but it does not make science creative as art is. Art is concerned with the communication between the artist and the spectator of experience personalised. Works of art are currency made out of subjective experience and communicated to individuals also perceiving them subjectively through their senses, and measuring them against their own experiences. But science is concerned with the development of theories and inventions objectively. The subjective element of the scientist's experience of, and feeling about, the objects is as far as possible an irrelevant factor. The scientist's intelligence is midwife of the objective process, bringing into the light the theory that derives from a previous theory. The standards which apply to this process are the demands of abstractions and things to be realised without interference from the subjective and personal nature of the scientist. This is scientific truth, truth neutral as nature, the truth of things, truth equally true to itself whether there is invented a machine to save mankind or one to destroy it.

Science is also, of course, a servant, and whether it is used for moral or immoral purposes depends on the will of man. But it is a servant that dwarfs man. It puts into men's hands enormous powers, and some of the men who have these powers seem to the students at all events, scarcely human.

The slogan of the Sorbonne students *'L'imagination prend le pouvoir'* expresses the wish of the students for a world created after their human image as against a world dominated by the politics, power and interests of the production of things. The whole emphasis of the students' movement is on individual life, challenging the machine. Diana Trilling in an article on the Columbia students,[1] points out that they call themselves 'existential'. By this they mean to emphasise whatever in them heightens their consciousness of being persons, since they feel that they live in a society which denies personality. To them the central value of living is life itself, enhanced by whatever actions or stimuli or relationships make the individual most conscious of his own existing. And they regard the leading figures in the political parties as totally unrepresentative of what they mean by life. If President Nixon is the centre, then they must be eccentric.

For evidence of this one does not have to look further than the newspaper reports almost any day of the week. For instance, in this morning's *The Times* (1 November 1968) the Washington correspondent, Mr Louis Heren, quotes a remark by 'one of Mr Nixon's close advisers a man wise in American politics'. It is that Mr Nixon was probably the last candidate of the pre-television era. In future, candidates would probably be selected by some central casting office with a computer programmed to match available men to the demands and fashions of the television age. On the same page of *The Times* we are told by another correspondent that 'disenchanted young Americans plan to launch a nationwide series of protests because they say the presidential election offers no choice'. In addition to marching through the streets and on to college campuses,

[1] Diana Trilling, 'On the Steps of Low Library', *Commentary*, November 1968.

protesting, the campaigners, we are told, tried to stage 'love picnics' and 'draft card burnings and release greased pigs in the streets. In San Francisco, Mr Jerry Yubin, leader of the Yippies (Youth International Party), has called on his followers to undress in polling booths, and put the drug LSD in drinking water.'

These tactics carry into political manifestations the earlier performances of dadaists and surrealists. They are the protest of those who feel that the society in which they live is activated by impersonal motives of power and interest and led by candidates, who seem like cut-outs made from cardboard. To draw attention to the contrast between personal being and impersonal dehumanised public behaviour the Romantic emphasises everything that is most personal, human, hysterical and even weak and absurd in himself.

One aspect of such demonstrations is that those who make them draw attention to their own futility. It may be that they feel that they can only make ineffectual protests. Yet the more the young feel that the society is inhuman, the more likely it is that there will be such protests. George Kennan remarks on the temperamental distinction between those who believe in order and those who believe in social justice. But if the kind of order which exists in the society is maintained by rulers who are selected on the basis of information fed into computers to answer the question who is likely to be the most popular candidate on television, then another distinction comes into play: which is that between those who think that man is made for the society of a Witches' Sabbath, and those who believe in a human Sabbath made for man. The rebellious students, with all their faults, believe that the Sabbath should be made for man – or at any rate for youth. And they fear that whoever ceases to be young, ceases to be man.

The University as Agora

The University City State

Today's students are entirely different from the Oxbridge, Harvard, Princeton or Heidelberg students forty years back. The term 'student' itself marks a change, for then we talked, in England at all events, of 'undergraduates'. The word student had about it a continental ring and seemed even old-fashioned – suggesting *The Student of Prague* or Heidelberg students drinking from richly embossed flagons, their faces scarred with arrogant wounds won in duels.

The 'student' was a continental concept and took one back to the students in Marlowe's *Faust*, or Goethe's play of the same name. Mention of this is not idle, because in fact the noisy, brawling, opinionated, diabolic-minded, theological students of those days correspond more to the idea of the student now emerging than to the rather juvenile undergraduate of the 1930s who had to be either an 'aesthete' or a 'hearty'.

To be an undergraduate then filled one with a feeling of prepubescent impotence. One had the frustrated sense that everything one did was 'undergraduate' stuff: undergraduate politics, undergraduate art, undergraduate falling in love. The walls did not shout, like those in Paris, May 1968, *qui ont la parole*, they looked and listened and merely whispered that everything an undergraduate did, from politics or poetry to religious doubts and suicide, thousands of much better and cleverer undergraduates had done in the past.

Looking at today's students, the old are inclined to say that in their day the university was the place of pure scholarship, detachment and refined cultivation. But just as there were scholars then, there are scholars today. And almost certainly the average student works harder today than the more or less amateur undergraduates did forty years ago. For one thing, the university has become more a knowledge-factory and makes more stringent academic demands. Forty years ago, undergraduates were divided into those who were scholars, those who were training to go into the professions, and those who went to Oxford or Cambridge, as to some dubious finishing school, to acquire the veneer of a gentleman. There was also the great division of manners between hearties and aesthetes.

Oxbridge undergraduates were on the near side of a stream beyond the far shore of which lay real life. They dwelt in a peculiar kind of void, like the souls in Maeterlinck's *The Blue Bird* waiting to be born. There were wonderful souls like the members of the Cambridge 'Apostles' or the president and other grandees of the Oxford Union concerning whom one asked 'What will he be Afterwards?' – well-knowing that he was a phantom now. He might become prime minister or an alcoholic or both. He would have acquired both skills at Oxford. But meanwhile he was kept in this box, like a piece in a game not in play, to be taken out for the Real Game later.

Today, though, with the vast increase in the student population; with students drawn from different social classes and an increasing proportion of them coming from the working class; with the lowering of the age of maturation since the war, and with a sexual freedom which was unknown among students a generation ago, the universities represent that half world which is under thirty to the other half which is over. They would perhaps be the more influential half if they were not blessed and cursed at the same time with a gift of the sort given to their favourites by ambiguously doting Greek gods. They are young and they may, while demanding power, pour contempt on the old, but they will cease to be students. A terrible dawn will arrive when the words *vieux crétin* spat from the contemptuous lips of some crapulous senior establishment figure will fall on their own heads.

But the universities are no longer the communities, half monastic, half secular, of forty years ago. Where there were institutions whose functions and disciplines it was possible to grasp, there are sprawling cities. Where there was one there are sometimes now four or five universities. The campus of a great modern American university, with its population of up to thirty thousand or forty thousand students is like a city state in which there are better and worse off citizens, new and old quarters, traditions and inventions and the most experimental trends. The University of California with its dozen or so campuses is like a country of city states, of which Berkeley is far the most important. It is to ancient Athens, as James Joyce's Dublin is to Ithaca.

Some years ago, I congratulated a friend of mine at the University of Michigan at Ann Arbor on his good luck that Ann Arbor was only a few miles from Detroit. He said: 'Ann Arbor doesn't go to Detroit, Detroit goes to Ann Arbor', and he started telling me of the programmes of theatre, concerts, lectures, conferences, festivals that take place each year on that campus.

The great American universities are producing their own culture. In some cases the arts are becoming transferred lock, stock and barrel to the campuses. Modern music provides a striking example of this. There is a tendency for the compositions of avant garde composers to outstrip orchestras (either because the work needs no orchestra or because it makes such complex demands that the orchestra cannot play it). Audiences in cities for the most part will not listen to recent avant garde music. Conductors and the older and middle generation of composers (taught at the academies and themselves teachers of composition) cannot teach it. In this situation the young composers go to the universities where there are the teachers of higher mathematics (from whom they need to learn), acoustic laboratories, computers and the electronic devices which they need for their compositions. There are also, among the students the instrumentalists and technicians prepared to learn new methods. Finally there is the intensely interested audience of the young who are preoccupied with the new and experimental.

There are parallels to this in all the arts. Notoriously, there is a migration of poets, from England as well as America, to the American universities. If you look at the biographical notes on poets contributing to any reputable magazine of contemporary American poetry, you will almost certainly find that over half the poets represented earn their living by teaching at universities. Some years ago it looked as if an extremely sophisticated new-critical academicism would be the result of this marriage of the campus to the muse. But the anti-academic poets, the experimenters in new forms, the psychedelics and the Yippies have now moved into the universities. They were until recently strongly entrenched at the University of New York at Buffalo, for example. The universities have moved beyond the stage of absorbing artists and making them into professors to a further one of giving them room on the campus to exercise experimental freedoms.

The university considered as city state includes different disciplines and functions, different attitudes; classicism preserved intact and kept living by its devotees, tradition concurrent with experiment, public debate with the most hedged in and protected private values, all these active and vivid as nowhere else. The model for it is not the Greek politicised community but rather Freud's famous metaphor (in *Civilisation and its Discontents*) for individual life, of a Rome in which all periods of the city's development survive concurrently side by side and sometimes one within another:

Let us make the fantastic supposition that Rome were not just a human dwelling place, but a mental entity with just as long and varied a past history: that is, in which nothing once constructed had perished, and all the earlier stages of development had survived alongside the latest. This would mean that in Rome the palaces of the Caesars were still standing in the colonnade of the Castle of S. Angelo, as they were up to its siege by the Goths, and so on.

It is a beautiful metaphor which Freud develops with knowledge and wonderfully consistent poetic logic, at considerable length. A university, which like the life of an individual represents all the stages of the development of civilisation, past and present, should be this: a collection of disciplines deriving from different historic epochs, with perhaps little conscious communication between them.

Today the university city state is a reflection of the students, many of whom come from different backgrounds and classes. They overwhelm the place so that they scarcely hear the echoes of the past.

A balance between the past of the university, embodied in brick and stones, gowns and silver, and the exuberant flesh and blood life of the students with *hair* (and both sexes dressed in blue jeans) cannot be maintained. It is weighted in favour of the

168

living contemporary fact, the students, who are the university. Previously it was reasonable to assume that the buildings of the older universities – with all they symbolise – influenced the students. Today, it would be truer to say that the students crowd out the buildings. All those slogans on the walls of the Sorbonne were the visible signs of the present scratching its name over the past and deleting its messages. Though doubtless there are some ears still attuned to hear.

All this is not simply the result of overcrowding and of there being new universities, and new buildings straddling hideously all over the old campuses. It also (and this is particularly true of England) results from many of the young people who go to the university coming from homes which are not of the university tradition. For the most part the sons are not those of fathers who went to the university: unlike children before the war who went to Oxford and Cambridge, Harvard and Princeton, already speaking the accents of the gown. Before the war the young received the stamp of the university on characters which were already wax to it. Today it is the university that is given its character by them (sometimes shocking to walls so old).

Another thing that makes the young today less impressionable is that they are *older* than their parents were at a corresponding age. It is generally accepted that a young person of eighteen today corresponds to one of twenty-one in 1939. Thus the university today, instead of overawing the students, tends to become the background of their 'scene'.

The university, in England and America makes a society that is more egalitarian than that of the nation that surrounds it. If they come from poor homes, the students are raised up to an average standard of the university which is more educated than their home, more civilised perhaps; if they come from what are called 'better' homes – bourgeois, that is to say – in many ways their standard is levelled down to that of the community of their fellow students.

Thus the university population, during the few years that the students are at the university, constitutes a kind of walled-in insulated community of the young, which resembles the kind of society one might expect to emerge from the Sorbonne 'Revolution'.

The idea that university education should be, as far as possible, available to the whole maturing population, became widespread after the last war. In India, Japan, the middle east and some European countries, notably Italy, near-universal university education resulted in large numbers of young people being qualified in skills for which there were no corresponding jobs. The students therefore rebelled against the society, and against the university, which had given them ambitions and intellectual status they could never fulfil in the society. Even in France a reason given for there being so much discontent among sociology students was the scarcity of jobs to be found after they had left the university.

Daniel Cohn-Bendit, in *Obsolete Communism: the left-wing alternative* cites a leaflet distributed on the campus at Nanterre, in March 1968, entitled: 'Why do we need sociologists?'

Students often ask themselves what jobs there are in sociology and psychology.

The facts are clear to one and all: there are many more students of social science than there are jobs waiting outside, and this even after elimination by examinations. The concern which students feel about their future goes hand in hand with the concern they feel about the theoretical position taken up by their lecturers, whose constant appeals to science only emphasize the confusion of their various doctrines.

From the realisation that when they left the university they would not find jobs, students went on to question the sociology they were being taught, and the attitudes of their professors towards teaching it. They formed the opinion that industrial sociology has been used as a weapon to help the world bourgeoisie and that in being trained as sociologists they were being enlisted – supposing that society provided them with the jobs – to do the same thing. Yet when they had expressed these attitudes they found themselves more interested in their studies than they had been before. In developing a critical attitude towards what they were taught, they could learn how to use sociology as a weapon against the society and against the university. But the university considered as a community is not a microcosm of the society, it is more advanced than it.

Although it is arguable that certain subjects which are taught with an appearance of objectivity are really taught in such a way that they make students conformist supporters of the society, it is also true that the structure of a great American university 'objectively' is as socialist as it is capitalist: and this despite the presence on the campus of those governmental agencies that may make it an instrument of bourgeois ideology.

To take only one example: in the conservative state of California, every young person with the necessary (and minimal) qualifications is entitled to university education at very small cost. The students are assisted by the university in finding part-time employment (sometimes on the campus itself), to help them pay for their education. They are able to borrow money from the state (which they can repay later) to support them-selves during the financially difficult period of their education.

On the campus the students look, and for the most part act like, members of a classless society. The foreign visitor finds it difficult at Berkeley, Columbia or Chicago to distinguish between most rich and most poor students. This of course conforms with the American custom whereby wealthy parents often limit their children to very small allowances. And in ordinary circumstances, when politics does not offer burning issues, the surface appearance of social equality has little effect on the students' attitudes, which may be those of their parents. But when crises arise such as the recent one of Vietnam, the fact that the campus is an island of egalitarian democracy suddenly becomes politically relevant. It was not difficult for the students at Columbia, regardless of whether they came from rich or poor homes, and regardless of colour, to make themselves into a commune.

We are often told that America is a classless society. But although it is obvious that it does not have class distinctions corresponding to those in Europe, this hardly seems an accurate description of a society in which the rich, the successful, the managerial and the governmental groups so clearly manipulate the others. But what is true is that the controlling groups emerge from a general sea of classlessness into which they may fall back (I am not concerned here with a few exceptional families and small local strongholds of aristocracy and plutocracy). The American campuses are places where the young have fallen back into the American classlessness.

171

And classlessness has become more and more a characteristic of students all over the world. This is true, despite frequent reminders that the students at the Sorbonne, and in West Germany, for example, are 'bourgeois'. They may be bourgeois at home but they do not look it on the campus. Although they come from bourgeois homes many of them feel de-classed at the university, and are pleased to be. They even regret that they are bourgeois, and want to bring in more of the young workers to join the community in which they have shed their class. During their demonstrations, occupations, liberations, etc., the students enjoy the experience of living in a revolutionary society without class. The university has become 'ours', occupied by us, taken over by us, abstracted from the authorities. Youth replaces class. The campus is the Revolution.

The reasons for the student revolts are to be found, usually, in the society, and not in the university. The students proceed from protesting about Vietnam, desegregation, the Third World, etc., to finding – or hunting out – things in the university which correspond to their grievances about the society. Sometimes these connections may seem tenuous, as in the example I quoted of Dr Krippendorf saying that in teaching eighteenth-century literature, a professor is helping the Americans in Vietnam. In the Fabian pamphlet on the universities, Mr Trevor Fisk quotes Mr Tom Fawthrop: 'It may seem a long way from the examination hall to the paddy fields of Vietnam,' but both are in fact simply symptoms of 'Western monopoly capitalism'. This is an example of the desire to interpret the class struggle and imperialism into all social activities, which seems to have survived intact from the Thirties.

All this does not mean that moving from their general social discontent to the particular situation in which they find themselves, of the universities, the students have not found things in them which need improving. There are bad conditions, the result of overcrowding, absentee professors, unfair examinations, lack of participation – all those things.

If allowance is made for the fact that dissatisfaction over the state of the world leads to dissatisfaction with the university, nevertheless the confusion of local, university issues with world-wide political ones seems self-defeating. For when the students are really concerned with some justified grievance which is to do with the university, it ought to be dealt with for its own sake, and not because it is symbolic of some quite other matter, such as the war in Vietnam. This is partly because if the authorities come to think that all grievances are symbolic of remote issues, they will also come to realise that there is no point in remedying them, since when a grievance is removed the students will simply go out in search of another – another symbol. It is partly too because if the students are persuaded that a fight over the examination system is really the same as one in a paddy field in Vietnam, then they may lose sight of the political issues in purely local ones which they take to be battles in a world crusade. Thus at a conference of art students I heard militants discuss matters such as their right to walk down some corridor reserved for faculty members with the same fervour as they discussed matters such as the H bomb.

Participation and Politics

The Critical University seems to be an idea which is doomed to failure. In practice what it means is abolishing the distinction between teachers and students, both of whom are treated as equals, while the subjects supposed to be taught dissolve into endless discussions of the reasons for, and approaches to, teaching them.

Participation, however, implies not the Critical University, but the university becoming continuously self-critical: debating its own processes and procedures. Experiments which have been made in some universities, and are under discussion in others, are student senates or parliaments to discuss university policy; student representation on committees arranging courses and examinations, even student representation on examining boards.

Ideally, the idea of a university in which there is a heightened state of awareness on the part of faculty and students as to the significance of what is being carried on seems good. In practice, there is the danger that participation will result in encouraging a busy-body type of student, like a school prefect, a seeker after office, who will make a career of sitting on committees and bossing other people, long after the present phase of generous

173

and sacrificial enthusiasm has passed. One of the paradoxes about the present generation of students who rebel against bureaucracy is that they themselves so often appear to be frustrated bureaucrats. The first thing they set up is a committee; the next, an office, with telephones, typewriters, etc.

If questions are asked about the ways in which certain subjects are taught, the attitudes implicit in teaching them, they should be answered, even if the answer is to explain that no answer is to be given. With some subjects, the question of an ideology or political or cultural attitude being insinuated into teaching does not arise. I cannot see that it does with the teaching of modern languages, for example, or with certain branches of science. Presumably the learner is learning these things for his own reasons. He regards a foreign language as an instrument which the teacher is putting at his disposal.

An example of the way in which the question 'Am I being brainwashed by the society when I learn this subject?' can arise is given by the attitudes of the Nanterre students towards their studies in sociology. I have already drawn attention to Cohn-Bendit's claim that sociology promotes the aims of bourgeois industrial civilisation. In his book he cites Mayo's methods of adapting the workers to the industrial machines, as an example to show that when he learns this, the student is being taught a technique for the exploitation of labour.

It might be said that certain subjects, if you view them in the context of the society in which they are taught, do give rise to questions of ideological attitudes which they might communicate. To take an example from psychology: one might view neurosis either as an individual or as a social phenomenon, if it arises from the failure of the individual to adapt to his environment. If one considers it as a purely individual phenomenon, then the problem of the analyst is to adapt the individual to his environment; if one considers it as a purely social one, one might think that the individual should not learn to adapt to his environment, since it is that which is wrong, and since his neurosis may be considered a protest against it. Or one might think that the patient should be cured of his neurosis in order that he may protest more effectively against the environment.

If questions of this kind are raised, they ought surely to be discussed. In fact, to the extent that students are critical of the society and suspect that they are being brain-washed by it, they do arise. On the other hand, little is learned if students spend too much time discussing the social significance of the subject rather than the subject itself.

Clearly a distinction has to be made between a subject considered as a compact self-contained packet of knowledge to be learned and its significance in a social or political or religious context. In teaching literature, questions may arise of the relevance of a writer's beliefs and political views to his work. The tendency of modern criticism is to treat these as though they were only to be considered in so far as they are elements which have been transformed within the work itself which is viewed as autotelic and separate from the beliefs, as from the biographical material, from which it has arisen. Thus most teachers would only discuss W. B. Yeats's esoteric religious belief and his political fascism as relevant to his poetry, to the extent that some knowledge of them contributes to an understanding of the poetry and independently of their religious or political implications. Yet Yeats believed strongly in these views and sometimes wrote poetry to express them. Some students might go to the poetry to discover the beliefs. In this case the poem, which has become as it were sterilised and insulated from the views and experiences out of which it arose, has to be connected with them again. Views which Yeats himself took seriously and which he expressed in his poems have to be discussed.

Teaching is in fact always based on certain assumptions, beginning with the perhaps optimistic one that the teacher knows more about the subject than the student. If there were no such assumptions nothing could be taught, there could only be discussion as to whether a subject was worth teaching or as to its political or social significance. This happens with the Critical University.

An assumption is the answer to a question which is taken as closed. Some assumptions however depend on hypotheses which, although they may be useful for the purpose of communicating knowledge, and getting on with the lesson, are so doubtful that they throw doubt on the information which is being conveyed. For example, a theory which rests on a whole string of dubious assumptions is that of the Great Tradition of English Literature which forms the basis of the teaching of

175

Dr F. R. Leavis and his followers. The basic assumption is that we are living in a modern period in which there has been a complete breakdown of the continuity of tradition in our fragmented society. The tradition existed when there was the unified culture of what is called the 'organic community' in which the social order, religious belief, arts and crafts all realised a shared and single view of life. Since this no longer exists the critical reading of such books as crystallise in their vision of life the organic community is the only means by which contemporaries can establish contact with the tradition. These works form the Great Tradition. There follows a great deal of debate as to what works fit into the canon. A theory of this kind can only have force if it is preached as a kind of dogma, subscribed to by disciples who really believe that such an order as the Great Tradition exists, and is infinitely superior to vulgar ideas such as the Six Foot Book Shelf or The Hundred Best Books. If they were not prepared to bow their heads in reverence when – for instance – the High Priest of the Cult declares that the only work of Charles Dickens to fit into the canon is *Hard Times*, the whole idea would seem arbitrary and rather silly.

The Great Tradition idea is worth mentioning because it illustrates the kind of teaching which is based on questionable assumptions. At first it is stimulating, because pupils are excited by the idea of the goals set by the Great Tradition. But later it proves merely inhibiting when they realise that it means simply that a list of books which they are supposed to prefer to all other books is being prescribed for them. It might be stimulating as a subject for discussion.

Just as terrible doubts about world politics have led students to see the university as a microcosm of the society, so doubts about such things as the uses to which scientific knowledge was being put may have led them to question the attitudes being transmitted to them by their teachers.

Thus, ideally, students should be on all levels as conscious as possible of the reasons for methods of teaching, and for the organisation of the university. A limitation on participation is however imposed by time. It is often forgotten how very little time there is in a university; for vice-chancellors, presidents,

176

administrators, faculty and students. Often what the students are complaining about, if analysed, might turn out simply to be lack of time to make arrangements which, if there were eternity to fill with talk, would be desirable.

The time-scale of the student's life at the university also rules out certain kinds of participation. It would be absurd for example (although nothing is so absurd that it is not endlessly discussed) for students to appoint professors. What makes it absurd is that if this were done, the professor's span of work time life would have to be segmented into sections of his being reappointed (unless indeed he was dismissed) by every student generation. Students might well, however, be consulted as to the appointment of teachers who are freelance: writers in residence, for example, or holders of the Chair of Poetry at Oxford University.

Apart from arrangements for direct participation, of students in committees, student parliaments or other assemblies which have various powers, there would certainly be more sense of participation if relations between teachers and students were improved, and if teachers were more accessible to students and treated more as equals. In many of the great American universities the structure of university organisation seems top-heavy and therefore inhibiting. Sometimes the faculty as well as the students feel excluded from the centres of the university. There is a tendency today for alliances to be formed between younger members of the faculty and militant students against president and administration: this is easily dramatised as an alliance of those who are alive against the computers.

The Study Commission which inquired into the disorders at Berkeley and which put forward various proposals for improving relations between the authorities and the students, reported:[1]

Discontent with the university is deepened by the degree to which the university's atmosphere reproduces the characteristics of the society. The university is large, impersonal and bureaucratic. The acquisition of specialised skills has often been substituted for the education of persons instead of supplementing it. Some of the most

[1] *The Culture of the University: Governance and Education*, University of California, Berkeley, June 15, 1968.

marvellous expressions of human dignity – the activities of learning, inquiring and sharing which are brought together in education are being dehumanised. 'Instruction' tends to usurp the place of inquiry; specialised 'training' gradually commences at ever earlier stages of education; and the tempo of education is stepped up to meet the pressure of enrolment, the resentment of taxpayers, and the competition with other technological societies for national supremacy in the space age. The result is that instead of the warmth and cordiality which are the natural accompaniment of learning, relationships tend to be remote, fugitive, and vaguely sullen.

The university is also reproached for two failures, described as 'crucial':

1, the failure to develop a student body which respects the value of the intellect itself and
2, its failure to order its activities according to its unique purpose of nurturing the intellect.

Some of this seems a bit over-generous in leaning over backwards to rationalise the complaints of rebels. I suspect that members of the university should not blame themselves too much if the 'student body' does not respect 'the value of the intellect itself'. After all, the university gets at the student when he is already comparatively grown, and if he does not respect the intellect before he gets there, it is scarcely the fault of the university. The home and the school (and the mass media) are more plausible candidates for blame.

However this passage does suggest that if the university were less top heavy, 'large, impersonal and bureaucratic' and if it were organised into smaller units, on a collegiate plan, there would be a greater sense of participation.

My deepest misgivings about participation of the students in university administration and teaching arrangements, are that I fear too much involvement of this kind may divert the students from the concern with politics which was the starting point of their movement.

It may be that their political activities have sometimes been ill-advised. What is important though is that the students have discovered themselves as a politically conscious community within the university 'City State': something corresponding to the ancient Greek 'agora', the marketplace where young men discussed politics and morals.

Their politics of the the non-political shows that they are concerned primarily with ends, and only secondarily with the means to attain those ends. When they become over-concerned with means they tend to get lost in the confusions of current political parties, trades' unions, etc., just as they may become lost if they permit themselves to become too involved in university arrangements and programmes.

It seems to me that their role really lies in drawing the attention of people to the problems of their generation, which are not just those resulting from their being on one side of the 'generation gap', but which are the problems of the future, the world of which they are already flesh and blood.

To clarify this, it would be better to speak not of the generation gap, but rather of an overlap of problems of the future with the day-to-day ones of the present. Today the future is like a time-bomb buried, but ticking away, in the present. Time-bomb is no mere metaphor, for it is literally the Bomb which is, literally, the future buried in the present. It is also literally, the younger generation, the generation of those children who are already the population explosion, as they will find when they have grown up.

So the young generation is not so much a 'gap,' as an overlapping of the future, burdened with problems, which to the old seem abstract, but which are built into the flesh and blood of the young.

They should be encouraged to interest themselves in the problems of their world, of the immediate future, which are probably insoluble within the political contexts of the older generation which are those of the struggles between East and West.

It must surely be clear that for these problems to be dealt with, some kind of leap into the future is required. Perhaps the deeper significance of the rebellion of the young is that they are aware of this.

The students are concerned with the future. They look not so much at the world of today as of a generation hence, the world of their children. I can best illustrate the significance of this with a hypothetical example:

Supposing that there were a meeting of the United Nations –

more than this, a meeting, if possible, of all nations – in which representatives of every nation discussed the kind of world they would wish there to be in thirty years' time, after their deaths. In discussing this as an *ideal* they would have to agree to postpone for the time being discussion on how to get there. Agreeing only that if they determined the goal they would then find the means. At such a conference no one would be concerned with his own interest. They would think about the world and the world's children. They would think primarily about the ends to be achieved: a world without war, not overpopulated, not divided into irreconcilable ideological groups; a world of which the greater part of the population was not suffering from poverty which in addition to misery was a threat to the security of all mankind. When they thought of the people in this world they would be thinking not of themselves but of their children and grandchildren.

The students, with their derided ideals, their outdated anarchism, represent such a conference of those who leap the present and concern themselves intimately with the future. They are not concerned with the means. Their instinct is probably correct when they refuse to produce a programme and when they abjure all existing powerful political groups and parties. The significance of their approach to the 'young workers' is not that they are going to the proletariat but that they are going to those who are young, like themselves, among the workers. The politically organised proletariat is, after all, a great interest, like the Communist Party and the Trade Unions. The students go to those among the workers who are disinterested, just as they are disinterested among the bourgeoisie.

One should probably think of their movement as that of the planners of a 'parallel world'. We do not know how to get there, but if it was proved to be a better world than the present one, science should provide the means. If they do not concern themselves with means, they might nevertheless concern themselves with certain immediate problems.

Not all students are concerned with these things. The problem of the militant students is essentially a minority problem. That it has arisen is due not, primarily, to the 'generation gap' (although there are circumstances in many countries today which force young and old into opposition), but to the decision of governments all over the world to make university education available to everyone who is able to fulfil certain minimal academic requirements, without distinction of class or wealth. This has meant that young people are under parental and social pressure to go to the university because it is the opening for nearly all careers, and because it has become a very widely accepted status symbol. It is true, of course, that in many countries to have qualified at the university is no guarantee of a job; but not to have gone counts as a disqualification.

So the university has become 'universal' in the very democratic sense that the education it provides has become the universal right of all young people who pass the necessary entrance examinations. This process is probably irreversible, for various reasons. One is that modern technological societies require a large pool of those who have received higher education to draw from. Another is that the future society of automation and computers will have problems of leisure and unemployment which will be alleviated by sending large numbers of young people to these city states of culture. Finally, any attempt to revert to the old idea of the university, where only the members of a privileged élite pursue their, mostly humanistic, studies, would seem retrograde in a way which is probably unacceptable both to democratic and authoritarian societies. The mass university has become a status symbol not only for the students but for countries: like space rockets for the two great powers, and airlines or dams for the small ones.

The only people who could effectively wreck the universities are the students themselves, and in some countries they have already done so. They may succeed in doing so nearly everywhere or they may secede from the academies and set up their own experimental or critical universities, in this way granting the wish of their most conservative opponents who want nothing more than that the universities should again become shrines of learning untainted by agitation.

It is, however, by no means impossible for the university to accommodate both scholars and revolutionaries: for it to become, as it were, an agora beside a citadel (or even an ivory tower). The essential requirements for this are that the militants should allow the non-political scholars to get on with their work, and that the academics should not regard as unacceptable

181

the presence on the campus of students who want to change the society in which they live and who agitate in order to achieve this end.

One does not have to think of traditionalists and militants working harmoniously side by side. One may, though, think of them as people with different attitudes, and pursuing different ends, who respect one another's existence and rights. My private image of such a university would be of a campus in which, in towers (ivory and ferro-concrete), and in rooms, and in quadrangles surrounded by protecting walls, the scholars led their unagitatory lives, and where a college could be as traditional as its senior and junior members wished; where there would be buildings in which students, who might or might not be interested in the politics of the world, the nation and the university, learned their skills; and in which there would be spaces, assembly halls, unions, where those students who were political activists would be free to use the university as a place where they might express their views – and where they would be free to go outside the university into the world of power politics and industry – so long as they did not disturb their neighbours' peace, wreck the installations, or use the university directly as a base for overthrowing either the university or society or both.

It is doubtless important for education to catch up with the needs of the technological society. This means that places of learning will become as utilitarian as society and swamped with technologists. But the warning delivered by E. M. Forster when King's College Cambridge was confronted with expansion should be heeded:[1] 'Whereas in business generally expansion may be beneficial, it is harmful to our business, which is to produce civilised people.'

It has to be admitted that producing civilised people is no longer the main task of most colleges. But within the scientising flood there can surely be protected islands of tradition. Here, paradoxically, the rebels might find themselves in partial sympathy with the traditionalists, for their revolt is against the lack of values of the impersonal technological society. The traditionalists, like the militants, are critics, though their criticism may be from different points of view.

[1] Quoted by Raymond Mortimer in *The Sunday Times*, 29 December 1968, 'E. M. Forster: The Art of Being Individual'.

The idea here put forward, that the militants should learn to study and develop and practise their revolutionary ideas in peace, is likely to meet with derision from them themselves. They will regard it as an attempt to cheat them of their revolution, which they want *at once*. But, whatever happens, they will not get it for a long time, and, if at all, when they have ceased to be young. The experience of the students at Columbia University and at the Sorbonne shows that if student militants halt the functioning of the university, not only do they produce a reaction against them from the conservative portion of society, but – and this is even more serious – having left their own walls and gone, physically or metaphorically, into the streets outside, they find themselves confronted by the professional politicians of the left who have no intention of giving place to vociferous bands of youths who have renounced their birthright – the university – not so much for a mess of pottage as for a pottage of mess. Students who attempt to revolutionise society by first destroying the university are like an army which begins a war by wrecking its own base.

Talk of postponing the revolution until one is of age, may, to the young, sound like thinly disguised reactionary or liberal propaganda. But a young person who says to himself: 'I intend to be a revolutionary until I am thirty, and then if society does not grant me my revolution I will take revenge on it by giving up,' is frivolous. And in fact a great many of the students do take this attitude. But, as artists well realise, anyone dedicated to carrying out a task can make no bargain with time, can set himself no time limit.

Thus the militant students should accept the university as their base. This means that they have to meet it on its terms, which are, largely, those of the authorities. They may modify the terms but they may not act in such a way as to threaten the existence of the institution.

The question arises of the terms on which the militant students are acceptable to the universities.

The first task of heads of universities is to safeguard the rights of scholars and academics, of those who are making the most effective use of the machinery which the university provides. But having assured this, they should surely recognise the existence of a whole new class of students, intelligent enough to have got into the university (where some of them greatly distinguish themselves), who are, nevertheless, not academics. These new students are activists, active-minded and active-bodied, but critical of the world in which they find themselves.

It seems to me that the protest of these students – their rejection of contemporary power politics and the values of a predominantly consumer society – is one with which many teachers have no fundamental quarrel even though they may not wish for 'the revolution' and may not care for the way the militant students go about things. Further, the participation of the students in attacking problems of war and armaments, of racial inequality, of the deterioration of the cities, of the pollution of the atmosphere, and of the destruction of the countryside, is more welcome than it is a nuisance. These are long-term problems, which most older people (including cabinet ministers) avoid thinking about. Governments are more and more preoccupied with immediate issues such as the balance of payments.

Students who are concerned with politics should be encouraged to participate in the world. Where universities, educational authorities, and, beyond them, governments, can help is in giving students access to evidence about the way societies are run. To some extent the students already have this. They need only to be told that their libraries and their teaching spread disinterested knowledge. The suspicions of students who think that the way in which certain subjects – economic, political, sociological and even literary – are taught is a form of brain-washing, can be answered by analysing the relation of the society to the ideas and material disseminated.

A radical way of enabling students to witness and study the conditions of the modern world would be to enable student representatives to be observers at meetings in which certain problems affecting their future environment are discussed: perhaps meetings of the United Nations, but also meetings of the World Health Organisation, and of United Nations' organisations in which problems such as food, population and illiteracy are discussed. They should be encouraged to study forms of society which approximate to their own social ideals: the kibbutzim in Israel, for example, where autonomous communities run their own industries and agriculture, and relate to

184

other communities and to the government from these 'bases'.

I do not mean that the young should be shown these things in order to approve the ways in which they are run. In fact I think there is not the slightest probability of their being 'sold' the World Health Organisation or Unesco, or Israel's kibbutzim. The point is that they should see what the problems are through the lives of those who are trying to deal with them. They should see for the purpose of judging and criticising. The most legitimate demands that the young can make on the old is that doors should be opened to them, that they should have the completest possible insight into the running of society: that they should grasp problems in order to be able to relate them in their real amplitude to the machinery of their own ideas and ideals.

There are certain matters in which the young may very well say that they cannot wait and where they may demand immediate action. These are matters in which they are far more affected than the older generation. First of all, the mass media. It is above all the young and the children of the young whose consciousness is being conditioned by these. Unless they protest against the programmes sandwiched between the advertising, a later generation may be too degraded by the mass media to have the will to protest. Secondly, it is the young who will be affected by the population explosion. The old are of course aware of the problem but they will not have to live with the populations of the year 2000. Therefore it is the young of all nations who, if they directed their attention to this, could combine with their contemporaries all the world over, to insist on action being taken about this problem which will condition all other problems.

Another matter which could primarily be the concern of the young is the destruction of nature and of animal life in the world. The older generation can view with complacency a world in which nature will be ruined, animal life destroyed, after they are dead. For the young it is a problem affecting their lives. The same is true of the pollution of the atmosphere.

In order to exercise pressure about these things the young must be an international pressure group. For this reason, I welcome their sense of their own youth, their existential awareness, their feeling that they incarnate the sense of life. Having gone so far it is disappointing that they have such limited inter-

185

national feeling. They easily permit themselves to be confined not by national boundaries, but by class and ideological divisions. They show little real inclination to enter into one another's situations. Thus the Western students stupidly dismiss the Czechoslovak students as bourgeois without making the effort to imagine themselves in the Czechoslovak situation. If the young all over the world made the double effort to cultivate the awareness of values of living which are revealed to them by their youth, and to interpret this shared awareness into the situations which separate them, then they might become an irresistible international pressure group.

The future – their world – is a subject of common knowledge. One does not have to look further than the statements of intellectuals, scientists, and even politicians to see this. A brief look at it was taken by Lord Ritchie Calder in a speech entitled 'Hell on Earth', reported in the British Press, 24 November 1968:

When scientists and decision-makers act out of ignorance and pretend it is knowledge they are putting the whole world in jeopardy. My concern is to conserve the human spirit not from the hell hereafter, but from hell upon earth.

Every young person who grew up during the atomic bomb testing had radio-strontium in his or her bones – the brand mark of the atomic age. The scientists had calculated that most radio-activity would dissipate in space. Now all they could say was 'Sorry chums'.

After discussing some of the effects of atomic waste dumped into the sea and buried underground which will remain active for at least 250,000 years, Lord Ritchie Calder goes on to say that by the year 2000 the world population will be doubled and that the world's largest city will have 1,300 million people. This links up with the remark of several American students to me that the cities of America were bound to be asphyxiated in their own noxious fumes. It seems to me that the questions Lord Ritchie Calder raises are exactly those which students should be discussing.

The world which he describes is one which exists already, growing up with the young, maturing with them, to be fulfilled in the ripeness of their time. The old of today will be dead by then, and on their side of what is called the age gap they do not seem to worry much about it. But owing to what I call the overlap of time, the young have to anticipate this world and prepare themselves in every way for it.

186

About the Author

STEPHEN SPENDER was born in London in 1909 and was educated at Oxford University. Together with W. H. Auden, Louis MacNeice and C. Day Lewis, with whom his work is most often associated, he helped to forge a new consciousness and style in English poetry.